Kelly Florentia was born and bred in north London, where she continues to live with her husband Joe. *HER SECRET* (2018) is her third novel and the sequel to *NO WAY BACK* (2017).

Kelly has always enjoyed writing and was a bit of a poet when she was younger. Before penning her debut, *The Magic Touch* (2016), she wrote short stories for women's magazines. To Tell a Tale or Two… is a collection of her short tales. In January 2017, her keen interest in health and fitness led to the release of *Smooth Operator* – a collection of twenty of her favourite smoothie recipes.

As well as writing, Kelly enjoys reading, running, drinking coffee, scoffing cakes, watching TV dramas, and spending way too much time on social media.

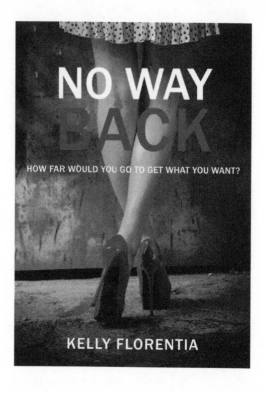

'a must-read for anyone who loves intelligent,
grown-up romance.'

Louise Douglas, bestselling author of
The Secrets Between Us

'A brilliantly-woven tale of love, friendship,
heartbreak and hope - I couldn't put it down.'

Jill Finlay, Fiction Editor of The Weekly News

When two eligible and attractive men are vying for your heart, it should be the perfect dilemma...

Audrey Fox has been dumped by her unreliable fiancé Nick Byrne just days before the wedding. Heartbroken and confused, the last thing she expects when she jumps on a plane to convalesce in Cyprus is romance. But a chance meeting with handsome entrepreneur and father-of-one Daniel Taylor weaves her into a dating game she's not sure she's ready for. Audrey's life is thrown into further turmoil when she discovers on her return to London that Nick has been involved in a serious motorcycle accident that's left him in intensive care. Distraught yet determined to look to the future, Audrey must make a decision - follow her heart or listen to well-meaning advice from family and friends? Because sometimes, no matter what, it's the people that we love who can hurt us the most...

The
Green Witch
Tarot Companion

About the Author

Ann Moura has been a practitioner of Green Witchcraft for over fifty years. She holds both a BA and an MA in history. Moura lives in Florida, where she runs her own metaphysical store, presents public rituals, and teaches classes on the Craft. Visit her at www.annmourasgarden.com or www.lunasolesoterica.com.

About the Artist

Kiri Østergaard Leonard (Brooklyn, NY) is a freelance illustrator who attended the Academy of Fine Arts in Aarhus, Denmark, before continuing her studies at the Pratt Institute in New York City. She has worked on art projects ranging from children's books to fantasy illustration. Visit her at www.kirileonard.com.

The

Green Witch
Tarot Companion

Ann Moura

Llewellyn Publications
Woodbury, Minnesota

FIRST EDITION

First Printing, 2015

Cover design: Ellen Lawson

Cover images: iStockphoto.com/32648686/©Elena Kalistratova
iStockphoto.com/25919769/©Borut Trdina
iStockphoto.com/23349592/©DavidGoh

Interior card art: Kiri Østergaard Leonard

Interior illustrations: Llewellyn Art Department

Llewellyn Publications is a registered trademark of Llewellyn Worldwide Ltd.

ISBN: 978-0-7387-4165-9

The Green Witch Tarot consists of a boxed set of 78 color cards and this book.

Llewellyn Worldwide Ltd. does not participate in, endorse, or have any authority or responsibility concerning private business transactions between our authors and the public.

All mail addressed to the author is forwarded, but the publisher cannot, unless specifically instructed by the author, give out an address or phone number.

Any Internet references contained in this work are current at publication time, but the publisher cannot guarantee that a specific location will continue to be maintained. Please refer to the publisher's website for links to authors' websites and other sources.

Llewellyn Publications
A Division of Llewellyn Worldwide Ltd.
2143 Wooddale Drive
Woodbury, MN 55125-2989
www.llewellyn.com

Printed in the United States of America

Other Books by Ann Moura

Mansions of the Moon for the Green Witch:
A Complete Book of Lunar Magic
(Llewellyn, 2010)

Ann Moura's New History of Witchcraft
(Seventh House, 2007)

Grimoire for the Green Witch:
A Complete Book of Shadows
(Llewellyn, 2003)

Tarot for the Green Witch
(Llewellyn, 2003)

Witchcraft: An Alternative Path
(Llewellyn, 2003)

Green Magic: The Sacred Connection to Nature
(Llewellyn, 2002)

Origins of Modern Witchcraft:
The Evolution of a World Religion
(Llewellyn, 2000)

Green Witchcraft III: The Manual
(Llewellyn, 2000)

Green Witchcraft II: Balancing Light & Shadow
(Llewellyn, 1999)

Green Witchcraft: Folk Magic, Fairy Lore & Herb Craft
(Llewellyn, 1996)

Acknowledgments

I am delighted beyond words that Llewellyn Worldwide has brought my vision of a tarot deck for the Green Witch into reality through the amazing talent of artist Kiri Østergaard Leonard. There are not sufficient words to express my gratitude for and admiration of Kiri's magnificent art and insightful suggestions for the interpretation of my card descriptions. Thank you, Kiri!

Many thanks also go to tarot editor Barbara Moore for her patience and her stunning discovery of Kiri; to art director Lynne Menturweck for her guidance, support, and hard work in the creation and editing of this project; to Carl Weschcke for inviting me to create a Green Witch tarot deck; and to all the Llewellyn family who contributed their time, knowledge, skill, and experience to bring this project into reality, especially Andrea Neff, whose keen eye for detail and creative suggestions made proofreading a breeze, Donna Burch for the terrific layout of the book design, and Ellen Lawson for the beautiful cover art. The level of cooperation, professionalism, and joyful accomplishment experienced by all in this project has been itself a work of art.

Much love and gratitude also goes to my husband for his helpful comments and support throughout the process, and to my daughter and my son for their input and encouragement.

Contents

Introduction . . . 1

Chapter One: The Major Arcana . . . 15

0–The Greenman 16

1–The Witch 20

2–The High Priestess 24

3–The Earth Mother 28

4–The Horned God 32

5–The High Priest 36

6–The Lady & The Lord 40

7–The Battle Wagon 44

8–The Crone 48

9–The Holly King 52

10–The Wheel of the Year 56

11–The Standing Stone 60

12–The Oak King 64

13–The Lord of Shadows 68

14–The Sidhe 72

15–Nature 76

16–The Wild Hunt 80

17–The Star 84

18–The Moon 88

19–The Sun 92

20–Harvest 96

21–The World Tree 100

Chapter Two: The Minor Arcana . . . 105

Pentacles 107

Athames 137

Wands 167

Chalices 197

Chapter Three: Spreads . . . 227

Witch's Circle Spread 229

Elemental Cross Spread 230

Wheel of the Year Spread 231

Mystic Pyramid Spread 232

Nine-Card Square Spread 234

Simple Yes/No Answer Spread 235

Tree of Life Spread 236

Conclusion . . . 239

Introduction

The Green Witchcraft approach to the tarot is based on a personal relationship to nature, earth magic, the elementals (earth, air, fire, water), and the power of the immanent Goddess and God in their many aspects, and to the faeries, spirits, and entities of the earth, otherworld, and underworld. The cards draw upon the seasons, sabbats, esbats, faerie lore, herbs, plants, animals, celestial energies, and the bounty of nature. As a tool for opening the psychic senses to these connections, tarot may be used for divination, guidance, personal growth, pathworking, meditation, and moving energy in magical works in a responsible manner for positive results. Tarot is part of living a magical life, knowing all are connected through Spirit and enjoying this ongoing contact with compassion and understanding, and remembering always the two major tenets of the Craft: "Love is the law and love is the bond" and "An' it harm none, do as you will"—ideals that should be reflected in readings, both personal and for others.

This tarot applies themes and motifs from stories of the Goddess and the God and the Wheel of the Year. The God has a triple aspect as Infant, Adult, and Elder. As the Oak King, he is the newborn Infant at Yule (Winter Solstice) and heralds the start of the light season. The Goddess has a triple aspect as Maiden, Mother, and Crone. At Yule the Mother births the God, and at Imbolc (February 2) she transforms into the Maiden as the infant Oak King changes into a vigorous youth and strong ruler of the wildwood. They unite at Beltane (Mayday) and rule as the Lady and the Lord of Nature. At Litha (Midsummer) the Oak King weds the Goddess, impregnates her, and transforms into the Holly King, the wise Sage, heralding the start of the dark season, which lasts until the Oak King is reborn at Yule and the Holly King departs. The patterns of the God are revealed in the Sun and the seasons of the earth, and during the dark season, the God is also the Leader of the Wild Hunt and the Lord of Shadows, ruling in the underworld. During the light season, the God is also the Lord of the Wildwood, the Horned God of fertility and power, and the Greenman who awakens the earth at Ostara (Spring Equinox).

The Goddess is the Maiden of Ostara, the pregnant Mother at Mabon (Autumn Equinox) who gives birth to the God at Yule, and the Crone of winter and the barren land. At Samhain (All Hallows' Eve) the Goddess and the God reunite in the underworld, the Land of Shadows, and make thin the veil between the worlds, allowing spirits to pass to and fro. The patterns of the Goddess are revealed in the lunar phases of waxing, full, and waning, and in the seasons of the earth, yet the roles of both Goddess and God are intertwined, for they are One Divine in Balance.

A Brief History of Tarot

The tarot is a deck of 78 cards generally read in a spread, or pattern in which the cards are laid out for a reading. Tarot readings have been associated with Witchcraft and magical practice for many decades and with Gypsy fortunetellers for centuries. Most people today agree that tarot cards arrived in Europe with Romany Gypsies migrating in the eleventh century from Rajasthan and Punjab in India westward through Byzantium and reaching Europe by around 1250. Playing cards are mentioned in writings from 1397 and 1441 as a game called *tarocchi*, similar to Trumps, Whist, and later Bridge; however, the earliest complete tarot deck of Europe still existing today was made in 1450 as a wedding present for the Viscount Sforza in Milan, Italy.

The Sforza deck has no titles or numbers for the 22 cards of the major arcana, and some cards correlate with Pagan traditions. The Fool is the Wild Man who awakens the earth at springtime in imitation of the Greenman; Apollo is the Sun; the tale of Diana and Orion reflects the power of the Goddess in the Moon, Temperance, and the Star; the Chariot is an Etruscan Battle Wagon controlled by the sheer willpower of a seated queen; Hercules is Strength; and the High Priestess is a Popess (Pope Joan) wearing the papal triple crown. The minor arcana consists of four suits (coins, swords, staves, and cups), with court cards of kings, queens, knights, and pages, and only symbols for aces and the cards two through ten, and thus no reverse meanings.

Pictures for all the cards evolved and changed to align with mainstream religious views. Reverse meanings for cards pulled upside down were invented in the eighteenth century by the French Mason Antoine Court de Gébelin and his salon of clairvoyants. Numbering, standardization of design, and interpretations evolved during the nineteenth and twentieth centuries through secret societies of Masonic ceremonial magicians. By the twentieth century, the most familiar form of the tarot was the

Golden Dawn's Rider-Waite deck. The 78 cards of the tarot are divided into two categories: 22 major arcana of archetypal cosmic powers and 56 minor arcana of daily life. The major arcana cards are numbered 1 through 21, with the Fool (Greenman) as zero. The four suits of the minor arcana are variations of coins, swords, wands, and cups, which in modern playing cards are called diamonds, spades, clubs, and hearts.

Green Witchcraft in the Tarot

This tarot deck utilizes images and energies associated with the Craft in nature and everyday life. Witches, male and female, young and old, are in the cards working and interacting with the elementals, the powers, entities, and beings of nature, the spirits of plants, the creatures of the earth, the faerie folk, the Goddess and the God of Nature in their many forms and aspects, the Moon and the Sun, and the universal energies of light, wisdom, and life force. The card images express the mysteries of the Divine, the key components of the present life path, and the activities, energies, and people of daily life.

The 22 cards of the major arcana are indicated by the numbers 1 through 21, plus the 0. They represent archetypes of cosmic influences, major energies, universal powers, and divine interaction. The Green Witch Tarot major arcana are as follows:

0—The Greenman
1—The Witch
2—The High Priestess
3—The Earth Mother
4—The Horned God
5—The High Priest

6—The Lady & The Lord

7—The Battle Wagon

8—The Crone

9—The Holly King

10—The Wheel of the Year

11—The Standing Stone

12—The Oak King

13—The Lord of Shadows

14—The Sidhe

15—Nature

16—The Wild Hunt

17—The Star

18—The Moon

19—The Sun

20—Harvest

21—The World Tree

Each card has a relevant main image plus an animal and a plant that contribute additional energy correlations to the meaning.

The minor arcana consists of four suits that relate to the elementals, seasons, cardinal directions, stages of life, and zodiac signs that can be used for personality types in court cards or the timing of events with aces. The suits of the minor arcana are the ritual altar tools of Witchcraft: the pentacle, athame (ritual knife), wand, and chalice, representing the elemental energies of earth, air, fire, and water.

Pentacles represent the element of earth, money, business, finances, physical matters, health, comfort, material things, possessions, challenges, rewards, winter, north, midnight, green/brown, the elderly, Taurus, Virgo, and Capricorn.

Athames represent the element of air, thoughts, intellect, strategy, plans, ambition, worry, decision, strength, power, fear, conflict, breath, communication, spring, east, sunrise, yellow/white, childhood, Aquarius, Gemini, and Libra.

Wands represent the element of fire, career, work, creativity, study, ventures, energy, action, ambition, life force, the self, summer, south, noon, orange/red, vigorous youth, Aries, Leo, and Sagittarius.

Chalices represent the element of water, emotions, intuition, love, friendship, relationships, psychic power, dreams, regrets, disappointment, fluids, autumn, west, sunset, blue/indigo, adulthood, Pisces, Cancer, and Scorpio.

Court cards are pages, knights, queens, and kings: pages (male or female) for children, young people, news, and energy; knights (male or female) for adult men or adult women, action, and direction; queens for mature or older women, and authority; and kings for mature or older men, and power. Aces are power cards for beginnings or new phases, the seasons, and major influxes of elemental energy.

The surrounding cards in a spread can influence the energy of any card, clarifying, explaining, or augmenting that energy. Having several of the same type of minor arcana card show up in a spread with ten cards or fewer gives additional insight into the reading, as shown here:

Ace–Beginnings: 2 = change at work/home; 3 = swift gains; 4 = new life

Two–Balance: 3 = talks with quick results; 4 = teamwork; reorganization

Three–Career: 3 = eventful time; deceptions nearby; 4 = determination rewarded

Four–Attainment: 3 = heavy workload; 4 = rest; strong foundation built fast

Five–Fulfillment: 3 = well-being; competitiveness; 4 = surprise confrontation

Six–Decisions: 3 = gains/successes; confusion; 4 = peace; evaluating

Seven–Change: 3 = contracts; friends' aid; 4 = slowed activity; disappointment

Eight–Communication: 3 = travel; quick events; trade; 4 = swift news; impulsive

Nine–New Paths: 3 = activity from communications; 4 = new responsibilities

Ten–Success: 3 = family celebration; 4 = commercial success; joy

Page–News: 2 = social activity/sports; 3 = good news coming; 4 = creativity

Knight–Direction: 2 = old friends; 3 = honors; 4 = swift action in vital issue

Queen–Authority: 2 = groups of women; 3 = influence; 4 = power of words

King–Power: 2 = groups of men; 3 = potential award; 4 = powerful contacts

Reversed Cards

A card is said to be "reversed" when the image is upside down from the reader's point of view. With 78 cards in the tarot deck, there are enough cards to conduct meaningful readings with all of them upright. Sometimes a normally positive upright card can have inhibited energy due to placement in the spread or surrounding cards, so the reversed meaning listed for the card could apply. Otherwise, the reversals can be read for those who prefer to mix up the directions of their cards while shuffling.

Reading the Tarot

In the Green Craft, everything is seen as connected in Spirit, so there is a spiritual communication with spirit guides, ascended masters, and the Divine, through which counsel and information may be passed to the inquirer (querent) by opening the psychic pathways of the reader. The reader comes into contact with a small portion of universal energy to address a question or problem, to gain guidance, or to find comfort. The tarot can provide a framework for opening a reader's intuitive senses to receive information, so the more familiar a reader becomes with the tarot, the more it can help increase the reader's psychic ability.

The cards do not tell the future, they do not control anything, and there is nothing scary about them. Their function is to provide a means for a reader to access the psychic intuition that is naturally present in all people but is more developed in some than others. They provide a focal point for visions, impressions, and energetic emanations surrounding a particular question or person as illustrated by the cards pulled. Because energy is always in motion, it can be moved, worked with, warded against, diverted, encouraged, or left to flow. For some people, simply seeing how the energies are currently aligned is sufficient for preparation. For others, the cards can be a useful source of direction, advice, and aid in making personal choices.

The meanings listed for each card in this book are intended as options and guides; however, personal intuition may also factor into any interpretation. Not everything listed for a card's meaning is to be used, but only that which applies to the reading. Prompt words are provided as a quick memory aid for the cards, and with practice it will become easier to remember fuller meanings and interpret them in relation to what is being asked or sought. Noticing a portion of a card that stands out or draws attention can indicate a special message or association in a reading.

Doing personal readings is good practice, but do not depend on the cards for every decision in life. Continued questioning on a matter can result in confusion or a lapse of psychic insight—better to wait a week or two before addressing the issue again. Asking for the prominent energy influence every day and pulling one card for the answer is good practice, but limit your readings for others to no more than two or three times per year so querents do not become obsessive about the cards. The cards offer guidance, but they are not a blueprint for every moment of daily life.

Readings should be approached with respect and kindness. Inform a querent that energy is always in motion and the cards show the energies currently active, the energies dissipating, and the energies approaching. Let the querent know that if what is shown is not acceptable, changes can be made—the energy can be prepared for or weakened with directed thought, worked around, or averted by changing outlooks, perspectives, behaviors, or planned actions. If the querent likes what is shown, the energies can be allowed to flow or can be enhanced with directed positive thought. A reading is good for up to about six months. A reading showing the major influence and event of each month in a coming year relates to how the energies are aligned at the time of the reading, allowing for changes to be made if desired.

The combination of assigned card meanings and psychic perception will vary with each reader, but confidence and trust in one's intuitive powers will grow with each reading. A querent may choose to contribute information during a reading, and this may offer confirmation to the reader of what is being addressed. If clarity is lacking for the reader, winging it is not an option. Either ask for confirmation or acknowledge that nothing is currently coming through in relation to the matter in question. Try reshuffling the cards and laying them out again. If the same cards or ones with similar meanings turn up, then that is what the cards have to offer.

Consecrating Your Tarot Deck

Consecrating a tarot deck prior to use creates an energy bond between the reader and the cards. Use a pentacle (this can be a piece of paper on which an encircled five-pointed star has been drawn), a bit of salt, lit incense, a lit white candle, and spring water (bottled is fine). Set the cards on the pentacle, and with hands cupped over them, say: "I consecrate this deck to my use through the power of the Goddess and the God." Pick up and fan out the cards and say: "These cards are consecrated through the power of the elementals: earth (*sprinkle a little salt on the cards and dust it away*), air (*pass the deck through incense smoke*), fire (*pass the deck quickly through the candle flame*), and water (*sprinkle the deck lightly with spring water and dry at once*)." Set the tarot deck back on the pentacle, and with hands cupped over the cards, say: "This deck is consecrated to my use. So mote it be!"

The cards may be wrapped in a cloth, placed in a pouch, or kept in a special box just for them. Herbs such as mugwort (for divination), sage (for clearing), or lavender (for positive energy) may be added, or a crystal of choice may be kept with the cards to aid in clearing or energizing the deck.

Ground and Center First

A reader should "ground and center" before a reading to avoid expending personal energy. This is done by focusing personal energy inward and releasing any chaotic or stressful energies down the body and into the earth, passing these through floors and foundations if necessary. Next, visualize roots extending from the bottoms of the feet, plunging deep into the rich, dark earth and pulling earth energy up to the top of the head. Envision cleansing and refreshing cosmic white light entering at the top of the head and cascading down the body to the feet, where it intertwines with the earth energy, and then both energies cycle back up the body to the head and back down to settle at the heart. Repeat the visualization whenever stressed or fatigued during a reading to be immediately reenergized. Pass the cards through incense smoke or white sage smoke after a reading to clear them.

Beginning a Reading

The reader can start by holding the cards and silently calling on spirit guides, ascended masters, the Goddess and the God, the elementals, and helpful entities for aid in giving a meaningful reading. Fan out the cards and give them a brisk wave to let elemental air clear them. Give the cards an initial quick shuffle and place the deck facedown on a table. Knock on the cards for personal readings, or have the querent knock on them, like knocking on a door. Place cupped hands above the cards and push the querent's energy into the cards while saying, "This is your deck." Pick up the cards and cut midway, placing the bottom portion on top, and hold a moment to let the energy cycle through.

Shuffle the deck and cut in whatever manner preferred, then restack to deal into a spread. Letting the querent shuffle the cards risks damaging the cards; however, the cards may be spread out on a table for the querent to select a certain number of them with which the reader will create the desired spread.

A querent may have a specific question or prefer a general reading, so ask before beginning the reading if there is something the person wants to address. When the cards are laid out in a spread, the card meanings are interpreted in relation to the question (if there is one), in relation to their positions in the spread, and in relation to each other. Sample spreads are provided in chapter 3.

Doing the Reading

The cards can be read by their surface meanings, by intuitive impressions, or by a combination of both. To use surface meanings, the reader must memorize at least a couple of prompt words for each of the 78 cards. Intuitive readings rely on psychic sight, which develops with use of the cards. Each card has multiple interrelated meanings and nuances, so select the meaning that relates to the question, the querent, and the other cards laid out.

When doing a reading, pull one card at a time, setting each in the appropriate place in the spread. It is customary to read each card as it is positioned or after all the cards are laid out, depending on personal preference. Read each card in relation to its location in the spread, as well as according to its meaning. A card in the past position is read as a past matter influencing the present, and so on. Try seeing the cards as flowing from one to the next in a series of energies or potential events, or as a story where one card leads to the next. Look for the common thread relating to the question asked, and if the question is not addressed, then the cards may have a different message to bring forward.

Keep an open mind and use the cards for guidance. Be tactful when addressing difficult topics such as illness, death, legal problems, losses, and relationship problems. Be honest but not authoritative or dogmatic. Remember that energy may be moved, manipulated, averted, and so on. Additional cards can be laid out for more guidance on a particular matter, for alternative actions that can be taken, and for more information on how a matter might evolve. Keeping a journal of personal readings helps to spot trends and developments, while noting which cards appear the most may give insight into important transitions. It is helpful to write down the cards pulled in a reading and personal impressions for later review, to gain new insights or confirmations.

More Uses for the Tarot

In Witchcraft today, tarot is used as a tool for divination, psychic readings, meditation, personal growth, pathworking, and spiritual insight. The tarot can be used in magical works as part of a spell by lighting a candle before a card illustrating a desired outcome. A relevant card can be placed under a candle holder, carried or placed in a significant place, or propped up for meditation. A card could be carried in a wallet, purse, briefcase, or pocket when asking for a pay raise (Six of Pentacles) or seeking employment (Six of Wands). A card could be placed over a doorway indoors when seeking changes (Wheel of the Year), clearing negativity (Ace of Athames), doing a ritual (High Priestess or High Priest), or doing a magical working (Star or World Tree).

Pathworking and meditation involve contemplating and examining the contents of each card over a period of time and receiving messages or insights from the imagery and characters. The major arcana can be seen as a progression of personal development, moving through the cards from a new beginning to a conclusion and another new beginning. The cards can help to evaluate a current condition and point the way toward enhancing spiritual, mental, and emotional development through meditation on each card. Keep a journal of impressions received to see how these evolve or change over time. When using a card for magical work, be careful not to damage the card, and when finished, clear it with incense and return it to the usual container.

Chapter One

The Major Arcana

0–The Greenman

This card represents the God of Nature in his aspect as the Greenman, historically depicted as a leafy male figure with a foliate face. He represents the fertility of spring and the awakening earth, when vegetation begins to sprout, early flowers poke through the barren ground, buds appear on trees, and there is hope for the end of the deprivations of the harsh winter. The Greenman has been impersonated since ancient times by men disguised as Jack o' the Green and Bushymen (covered in leaves), Burrymen (covered in dried burdock flower heads), Morris dancers (wearing bells), Wild Men (in hides), Fools (in tatters), and others in various cultures throughout Europe.

The Greenman is believed to watch over his imitators with approval and pass the energy of fertility to the earth through his surrogates to awaken the earth from winter's sleep, bless the land, and encourage fertility in crops and livestock through the ancient ritual of sympathetic magic. The disguised impersonators continue this tradition in modern-day festivals, dancing and striking the earth with a staff as they travel to farmsteads with a troupe of helpers and musicians, their festive mood enhanced with ale and other spirits throughout the day. At day's end, the staff is secretly buried and the disguises put away or burned.

The Greenman relates to the sabbat of Ostara, the Spring Equinox, when the God's energetic enthusiasm initiates new things, new beginnings, adventure, and growth. This card demonstrates the raw energy of nature, the joy of life, and the awakening of the spirit to a new adventure, awakening Mother Earth for the Goddess as Spring Maiden. This potentially chaotic energy should be directed with caution and thoughtfulness so it is not wasted. The zeal of this card may border on recklessness, and the querent is reminded not to take this energy to extremes, for there are always consequences to actions. If indicated in the spread as a departure from the routine, this card could represent something as minor as a vacation or as major as a change of lifestyle.

Mugwort, symbolizing fresh starts, fertility, and magical power, grows near the bench. A white dog, signifying support, fertility, and growth, leaps with the dancer.

Meaning: A fresh start, new beginnings, enthusiasm, excitement, spontaneity, courage, potential, creativity, fertility, innocence, innovation, vacation, primal energy, fearlessness.

Reversed: Recklessness, inactivity, continuing a project, unfocused energy.

Prompt Words: New beginnings, enthusiasm.

*Notes:*_____

_____

_____

_____

_____

_____

_____

_____

_____

_____

_____

_____

_____

_____

_____

_____

_____

_____

_____

_____

_____

_____

_____

_____

_____

_____

1–The Witch

This card shows the Witch as a confident, middle-aged woman practicing her Craft in the open air and through the four elementals represented in her tools: the wooden pentacle for earth, the athame for air, the wand for fire, and the chalice for water. She works with these powers and with the objects of nature to raise and direct energy for achieving her personal goals. The elementals are part of her communication with nature through magical ritual, and she conserves her personal energy by drawing upon her kinship with them to accomplish her goals. The Witch uses her knowledge, skill, and experience to achieve her potential while working her spells in harmony with the elementals, the Divine, and the powers and entities of nature.

Her cingulum is the ritual belt of white, red, and black cord representing the Triple Goddess as Maiden, Mother, and Crone. It is knotted with the measurements of the Witch taken when she began her path, and indicates her comfort in the Craft of the Wise. Her necklace of amber and jet beads reflects the power being called upon and the connecting of the energy to accomplish a task. She has cast her circle and purified it with a barrier of salt so that no unwanted energies interfere with her spells as she walks between the worlds.

The Witch takes control of her own destiny with a sense of responsibility and awareness that she use her skills with wisdom and honor, harming none. Honesty toward the self and others is necessary when working through and with the elemental energies, especially in public activities such as consultations, lectures, public relations, and any type of media expression. This card shows that self-confidence and communication are part of the process for raising and directing energy to achieve a goal.

The Witch conducts her Craft within the magical tradition of utilizing correspondences and adhering to ethical rules. The plant she is adding to the cauldron is ginger root, for success and swift action. A crow, representing magic and manifestation, watches from a branch of a nearby hazelnut tree.

Meaning: Controlling personal destiny, communication, opening up to a wider audience, power to make changes, skills for achieving goals, practical use of knowledge, originality, problem solving, initiative, creativity, originality, adaptability, diplomacy.

Reversed: Unconfident, blocked expression, hesitant, vacillating, guile.

Prompt Words: Taking control of one's personal destiny, skillful, astute.

*Notes:*_____

_____

_____

_____

_____

_____

_____

_____

_____

_____

_____

_____

_____

_____

_____

_____

_____

_____

_____

_____

_____

_____

_____

_____

2–The High Priestess

This is the card of the High Priestess enacting the ritual of drawing down the Moon during an esbat within a megalithic stone circle. She infuses the water in her cauldron with the power of the Goddess in her Full Moon aspect by drawing in that energy. The water can later be shared with her community as holy water for ritual acts of blessing, consecration, manifestation, abundance, divination, healing, cleansing, and purification. The High Priestess is knowledgeable in the ways of magic and the spiritual connection with the Goddess and the God, gaining understanding and intuitive comprehension of the unity of nature through her direct contact with the Lunar Goddess at the esbats. Her community trusts her wisdom and seeks her advice and help in their daily lives. She understands the secret mysteries of the Goddess and carefully chooses who she will take as an apprentice to teach, for the mysteries and arcane knowledge are shared with discretion.

The High Priestess works her magic rite within the sacred circle while the Moon's reflection shimmers within her cauldron. Her ritual robe with silver moonflowers embroidered on the sleeves, silver bracelets, amber and jet necklace, knotted cord of white, red, and black, and silver circlet depicting the Moon in its waxing, full, and waning phases are all emblems of her training in the magical arts for the benefit of her community. She trusts her intuition as a gift of the Goddess and uses it to open the gateway to wisdom so that she may discern the appropriate path to follow for further enlightenment. The Full Moon is a time for the manifestation of magical works and for divination, and the esbat rite opens the psychic senses of the High Priestess to union with the Goddess, from whom she gains insights to be shared with the community and refreshment of her spirit.

The High Priestess drops acacia flowers into the water for consecration and psychic power, and directs the lunar energy with her wand. Her black cat, a symbol of focus, magic, and psychic power, sits nearby watching the cauldron.

Meaning: Trusting intuition, insight, secrets revealed, keeping a confidence, perception, hidden truths, occult studies, destiny revealed, psychic dreams, psychic ability, being between the worlds, receiving divine inspiration, spiritual development.

Reversed: Clouded insight, discretion needed, ignoring intuition, shortsighted, vanity.

Prompt Words: Secrets, intuition, psychic ability.

*Notes:*_____

_____

_____

_____

_____

_____

_____

_____

_____

_____

_____

_____

_____

_____

_____

_____

_____

_____

_____

_____

_____

_____

_____

_____

3–The Earth Mother

The Earth Mother, pregnant with the God, walks the fields of grain carrying her cornucopia overflowing with the fruits of the harvest. She represents the fullness of nature, robust, healthy, and abundant. She can indicate a pregnancy or conception, but also growth, development, and matters coming to fruition or potentials in the process of becoming manifested. In ancient Rome she was the popular Goddess of Abundance, depicted on buildings and public fountains with her overflowing horn of plenty. The Earth Mother is the Goddess of Grains and Harvests, generous with her bounty. She represents unity with the benevolent aspect of the Earth Mother and enjoyment of her comfort and love in a time of plenty and peace. Her blue gown is the color associated with both the Goddess and good health. Her staff is held as a scepter with stalks of wheat tied to it, showing that her power is in the land and she is the very earth upon which all depend for survival.

This card relates the Goddess to the sabbat of Litha, the Summer Solstice. She is impregnated by the Horned God, and he turns his face to become that of the Sage, the Holly King. The Earth Mother holds the promise of life renewed within her, offering sensitivity and intelligence for communication between the worlds. Her influence can be felt in matters of self-expression, the start of a creative enterprise, and domestic contentment. Depending on the question or the surrounding cards in a spread, she can indicate marriage and pregnancy, or an understanding tempered with a gentle spirit. In her fullness there is expectation, hope, and satisfaction. The wreath on her head shows that she is part of the cycle of life, and here she is in full flower. Her own fruit, on which the world depends, is ripening within her, for her babe will be the Yule child, the Oak King reborn, opening the way from winter to spring.

Wheat fields and ripened grain on the Earth Mother's staff are symbols of wealth, fertility, and good fortune, while the flock of ducks that accompanies her represents abundance, prosperity, and fertility.

Meaning: Abundance, fertility, inspiration, emotional fulfillment, harmony with nature, growth, development, a project nears completion, folk magic, robust health, intellect, domestic joy, security, beauty, sensitivity, pregnancy, fruitfulness, motivation, sensitivity.

Reversed: Unrecognized potential, blocked creativity, vacillation, slow progress.

Prompt Words: Abundance, fertility.

*Notes:*_____
_____
_____
_____
_____
_____
_____
_____
_____
_____
_____
_____
_____
_____
_____
_____
_____
_____
_____
_____
_____
_____
_____
_____
_____

4–The Horned God

The antlered God of Nature stands in the forest clearing surrounded by the wildlife of his domain. He is the ruler of the forest and Lord of Beasts, a robust figure of authority, wisdom, and fertility. His power derives from his personal drive and leadership skills, but is tempered by his acceptance of the responsibilities that come with his position, for he is guardian of nature, the protector and nurturer of the natural cycles of life under his care. He also knows that he is part of this cycle, and he willingly plays his role through the seasons as he perpetuates the nourishment of the earth by his marriage to the Earth Mother at the summer solstice. He impregnates her, surrendering his virile energy to her care as he turns into his Sage aspect.

Now, however, he is strong, aware of his power, yet kind, gentle, and generous with his abundance. The Horned God is honored as benefactor and protector, yet he is also the Wild God of the Hunt, reflecting a time when hunting game was a necessity for survival. Indeed, his image as the Hunter can be traced back through time to ancient cave paintings of the antlered and hide-robed shaman working his magic for a successful hunt. The Horned God is master of the woods, the vegetation of the earth, and the animal kingdom. He builds and rules his domain in all the wild places, yet he demonstrates the life cycle within the changing seasons. He is compassionate to the animals that live out their roles as prey and predator, game and vermin, each according to the nature of their kind, for he teaches that the Divine Spirit dwells in all things. The Horned God reminds the hunter to offer blessings to the hunted with the understanding of the unity of all things in the ecosystems they inhabit, for what may be vermin to one may be sustenance for another.

Wild bergamot—representing authority, power, fertility, and energy, blooming with red brilliance, the color of blood—grows in profusion around the God. Ravens, symbolizing messages, guardianship, growth, and guidance, circle overhead while one of them whispers news of the world to the Horned God.

Meaning: Accomplishment, leadership, skills, responsibility, authority, personal power, stability, self-confidence, experienced, initiating plans, building projects, protecting what is created, fertility, satisfaction, husbandry.

Reversed: Bureaucratic, inflexible, indecisive, petty.

Prompt Words: Responsibility, builder.

*Notes:*_____

_____

_____

_____

_____

_____

_____

_____

_____

_____

_____

_____

_____

_____

_____

_____

_____

_____

_____

_____

_____

_____

_____

_____

_____

_____

5–The High Priest

The High Priest of the community wears the circlet of a solar disk as he stands within the stone circle and conducts the ritual of drawing solar energy and the power of the God into a basin of water. He directs the energy through his athame in one hand to create holy water, while he raises the other hand in blessing. Crystals pointing outward surround the basin, radiating solar energy and cleansing the sacred space and blessing the community beyond. Later, the sanctified water may be used for spiritual purposes, ritual, clearings, and empowering magical works.

This is a card of tradition and organization of spiritual practice such as is found with a Book of Shadows. The ritual is formulated for honoring the God, but also for guiding power and magical energy through ceremony for incorporation into all aspects of daily life. Magical practice is codified and established so it may be passed on to future generations through instruction and ritual celebrations. In many Pagan traditions, the roles of Goddess and God are associated with the Moon and the Sun and are portrayed in ritual by the High Priestess and the High Priest. Together they represent the Divine in balance, and each contributes to the cohesion of the community.

The power of structure creates a comfortable and familiar routine in which conforming to the social norms imbues a sense of peace and common ground for all in the community basking under the beneficent Sun. Excessive individuality can be like solar flares: dangerous, uncontrolled, and disruptive. As such, the High Priest is a figure of authority in spiritual matters, one who has studied and been trained in the teachings and ritual practices for his community role. This card infers the influence of organization in the elements to avoid financial loss in earth, mental struggle in air, career chaos in fire, and emotional distress in water. By working within the structure of the Solar God, the energy is controlled and security ensues.

Yarrow, representing the God, authority, blessing, energy, and protection, is on the altar and grows in profusion within the stone circle. A swallow, for the Sun God, community, and security, flies overhead.

Meaning: Working within social/cultural customs, organization, routines, formats, schedules, security, transmitted teachings, inspiration, rites and ceremonies, codifying spiritual insights, scholarly pursuit of spiritual understandings.

Reversed: Dominance, rigid attitudes, manipulation, disruption.

Prompt Words: Organization, structure, conformity, mentor.

*Notes:*_____

_____

_____

_____

_____

_____

_____

_____

_____

_____

_____

_____

_____

_____

_____

_____

_____

_____

_____

_____

_____

_____

_____

_____

_____

_____

_____

6–The Lady & The Lord

This card shows the harmony between the Goddess and the God, working together, making choices and decisions together with a unity of heart and mind. This partnership infers a conscious decision in which the intellect works with the emotions. Here the deities are united by their mutual interest in the hunt, each with hound and weapons of choice. The Goddess wears a circlet with her symbol, the silver horned moon, while the God wears a circlet with his symbol, the golden sun disk—Moon and Sun working together to benefit Earth, for without the Moon, there would be no tides, and without the Sun, there would be no life. Her silver bracelet shows the wisdom of the snake, while his golden ouroboros armband, depicting a snake with its tail in its mouth, shows the cycle of life reflected in nature and the galaxy. They acknowledge their cosmic roles as well as their earthly roles in the cycle of life carried out willingly, relating the card to Beltane and the May Day union of the Goddess and the God in partnership.

Choices in life may be driven by desire, ambition, preference, or necessity, but they require a clear idea of priorities. The presence of this card in a spread indicates that a decision needs to be made, and if it is not, the choice may fall into the hands of another. Many times this relates to deciding whether a person will make a good partner in life or choosing between two potential partners. Accepting emotional ties shows a willingness to experience a transformation that takes place through trust. There are new opportunities for growth through commitment, as well as a need for loyalty to and from the chosen partner, a need for mutual agreement and respect.

The Lady and the Lord of Nature stand before a large oak tree, representing truth, wisdom, and loyalty, and sacred to both the Goddess and the God of Nature who were venerated in oak groves in ancient times. Their hounds represent and accompany the Goddess and the God in their aspects of Huntress and Leader of the Wild Hunt.

Meaning: Decisions, partnership, trust, balance of opposites, careful consideration of choices, collaboration, harmony, commitment, love despite differences, loyalty, emotional ties, camaraderie.

Reversed: Dilemma, indecision, procrastination, worry.

Prompt Words: Decision needed with a partner or about a partner.

*Notes:*_____

_____

_____

_____

_____

_____

_____

_____

_____

_____

_____

_____

_____

_____

_____

_____

_____

_____

_____

_____

_____

_____

_____

_____

7–The Battle Wagon

The chariots of the Etruscans and the Celts were four-wheeled battle wagons, large and unwieldy, requiring a driver to handle the horses and take the warrior on board where he wanted to be on the battlefield. In this card, the rampaging horses have no reins and are instead controlled by the personal power of the warrior. He has the ability to command opposites and manage their divergent energies so they work together to accomplish his goals. This can be related in the business world to the one who takes charge and brings the team together to work on a project successfully despite their differences.

There is personal achievement through focus on goals, self-discipline, and leadership ability, with actions that bring swift results, whether in business, career, or personal objectives. Taking control and consolidating power for success is indicated here, and drawing together opposing personalities to work in unison for a purpose brings recognition and praise for one's merit. Balance is maintained by strength of will and management of energy.

This card indicates that a person has the ability to take control, be assertive, and handle the difficult situations that arise in life. Overall good health and strength of body, mind, and spirit are also implied in this card, and surrounding cards can help clarify the bearing of the Battle Wagon energy.

The Battle Wagon may relate to business travel with the potential for far-reaching importance. New projects could begin based upon previous successes, and there is a responsibility to live up to expectations. This card reassures the person that the capability is there; it only needs to be utilized, and recognition for a job well done will follow. Military service or a work-related domestic move could also be indicated with this card.

The key is that energy can be successfully raised, consolidated, and directed by the person to achieve desired goals in whatever matter or field involved, bringing victory and esteem for the individual.

The victorious warrior of this card is crowned with a circlet of woodruff, symbolizing success in battle. A magpie, representing battlefields, willpower, and balance, flies near the cart.

Meaning: Victory, merit recognized, successful action, self-confidence, personal achievement, leadership, consolidation of power, balance, control, dominance, conquest, good health, business travel, military service, relocation.

Reversed: Inaction, indecision, impatience, unrealistic goals, incomplete work.

Prompt Words: Victory, recognition of ability, business travel.

*Notes:*_____
_____
_____
_____
_____
_____
_____
_____
_____
_____
_____
_____
_____
_____
_____
_____
_____
_____
_____
_____
_____
_____
_____
_____
_____
_____

8–The Crone

This card shows the Goddess in her aspect of Wise Woman, or Crone. She walks in the light of knowledge and experience, and rests her hand on the mane of the lion, the symbol of the zodiac sign Leo, ruled by the Sun. The Crone shows that one has the inner strength to overcome obstacles through sheer willpower and determination. With courage and self-control, the greatest difficulties can be surmounted.

This is a card of power and energy, encouraging self-confidence and conviction of one's own ability to take control of a situation and bring it to a favorable resolution. By having fortitude and self-assurance, one may control and vanquish opposition and obstacles. Any darkness is a passing matter, and any period of difficulty may soon be resolved by steadfast resolution for the necessary rebirth to be achieved. By enduring the transition time with inner strength, better times will manifest.

This card also shows that love conquers all. The Crone and the lion walk together at ease as companions, strong and wise, looking out for each other on the road of life, so there is an indication of commitment and power applied gently. As such, inner confidence and fortitude may allow one to be a peacemaker or to exude an aura of calm that offers encouragement to others who are struggling with adversity. Being true to oneself allows one to remain composed and serene in the face of difficulties.

When appearing in a reading, the Crone reminds one that this inner strength is a wellspring within the individual, that it is part of that person and will never be used up, but may be tapped into whenever needed. Like the Witch's circle, wherein energy is gathered and controlled before being released to accomplish a goal or disperse negative influences, the interaction of the lunar Crone and the solar lion demonstrates the union of wisdom and inner power that will see one through any difficulty with composure and peace. The Crone has a staff to which is tied a bouquet of angelica, representing power, strength, and the sign of Leo. Beside her walks the lion, symbolizing authority, power, and strength.

Meaning: Fortitude, inner strength, self-confidence, courage, overcoming obstacles, perseverance, control, willpower, self-discipline.

Reversed: Weakness, emotionalism, compromise, boasting, overbearing.

Prompt Words: Fortitude, willpower.

*Notes:*_____

_____

_____

_____

_____

_____

_____

_____

_____

_____

_____

_____

_____

_____

_____

_____

_____

_____

_____

_____

_____

_____

_____

_____

_____

9–The Holly King

This card symbolizes the wisdom that comes from time and experience, and the need to discover one's own path. Here the God is seen in his Holly King aspect, the Sage who at Yule turns over his hourglass of wisdom to the newborn Oak King. The sack over his shoulder contains the gifts of knowledge and experience to be passed along to others. This is the wise mentor teaching others, the accomplished elder craftsman training the young, imparting to them the foundation that will support them as they gain hands-on experience. The lantern of the Holly King hangs from his stang, the two-pronged staff that is also an altar, and it continues to light the way for others. This new path offers change for others through example and by opening up new vistas, yet each individual learns on personal terms. In the passage of time, it is the trek itself that leads to wisdom.

Adaptation to the new is also indicated by this card, showing growth, evolution of thought, and understanding. A person may feel a need for introspection to contemplate their path or consider what it is that truly draws them. Spiritual questing may be involved, or disconnecting from the expectations of others. In finding a new path, one could be a beacon of encouragement to others, opening the way into new life patterns and progressing with inner development.

The figure of the Holly King is also that of Father Time, the old year giving way to the new year's infant in the renewing cycle of the seasons. The wise old God departs with a smile to his younger self, the Oak King, nursing in the arms of the Mother Goddess. Just as the old solar year ends and the new begins at the winter solstice, the cycle of life and lessons learned will be repeated through human generations as it is yearly for the God.

At the top of his bundle can be seen the tip of a small fir tree, representing life, spiritual development, light, and peace. The Holly King is accompanied by a reindeer, symbolizing knowledge and guidance.

Meaning: Seeker, introspection for enlightenment, forging a new path, personal growth, self-exploration, finding or being a mentor, wisdom comes in due course, prudence, discretion in sharing wisdom, progress, contemplation, guidance by example.

Reversed: Impulsiveness, imprudence.

Prompt Words: New path, wisdom, discretion.

*Notes:*_____

_____

_____

_____

_____

_____

_____

_____

_____

_____

_____

_____

_____

_____

_____

_____

_____

_____

_____

_____

_____

_____

_____

_____

10–The Wheel of the Year

This card shows the seasons of the year as the sabbat quarters of Yule, Ostara, Litha, and Mabon, along with the sabbat cross-quarters that occur in between those solstices and equinoxes: Imbolc, Beltane, Lughnassadh, and Samhain. Presented as an old-fashioned gaming wheel, the Wheel of the Year is always in motion, meaning that change is inevitable. The needle pointing to Yule emphasizes that transition moment from the dark season to the light season, suggesting improvement in one's circumstances. Just as the seasons are not under our control, there are some things that are simply a matter of luck. When this card appears in a reading, it could indicate the beginning of a long-term upswing of good fortune, lasting up to six months, same as the light and dark seasons of the ancient world. Other cards in a spread may show what triggers this energy or what area of life is being affected.

This is nature at the primal level, where fate may be linked to chaos and chance, allowing a person to benefit through events beyond their control. The actions of others or unexpected events may prove advantageous, offering a lucky break. Since the Wheel is always turning, accept and enjoy the good luck when it arrives, for like the seasons, this energy may wane. The passage of the sabbats through the year offers possibilities and opportunities with each new phase, so this could indicate the beginning of a new cycle in one's life. There may be surprise events, transformations, or unexpected success. Impediments could suddenly vanish, allowing for advancement, positive developments in one's situation, or finding solutions to problems. This card also indicates potential for a good outcome to a project or trying new ideas while still being true to one's inner vision. A card of encouragement, the Wheel of the Year often turns up in a reading to show a person is on the right track with energy for unexpected progress.

At the base of the Wheel's pedestal grows an abundance of basil, representing luck, energy, and the deflecting of negativity. A hawk, symbolizing empowerment, fearlessness, and the life force, flies near the wheel.

Meaning: Upswing of good luck, success, trying new ideas, destiny, fate, help comes quickly, advantageous surprise, progress, improvement, opportunity, transition, transformation.

Reversed: Small gains, short-term success, recklessness.

Prompt Words: Long-term good fortune, sudden progress.

*Notes:*_____

_____

_____

_____

_____

_____

_____

_____

_____

_____

_____

_____

_____

_____

_____

_____

_____

_____

_____

_____

_____

_____

_____

_____

11–The Standing Stone

Standing stones are symbols of authority, boundary markers, and monuments. As objects of power and balance, unyielding and strong, blending earth and spirit energies, they once formed a meeting place where people in a community could decide issues and settle individual disputes before the gods. In this circle of smaller stones, a community council could sit in arbitration or discern justice, hearing evidence and rendering a decision. The tradition of engraving stone obelisks and tablets with the laws of a society relates to the power of the megalith and here symbolizes concepts of Craft practice. The stone has been carved with the triquetra symbol of the Triple Goddess, the scales upon which the facts of a matter can be weighed for a balanced and impartial decision, the Craft ethic of "harm none" for fairness and compassion, and the labyrinth signifying the path one must follow to reach the heart of the matter and find truth. The path leading to this circle of stones passes through the dark forest, and yet the light of truth shines through the trees to illuminate the stone and ensure that the truth of the matter will be revealed.

Objectivity is emphasized when this card appears in a reading. The Standing Stone shows that one has gathered information and fairly evaluated a matter, and may therefore trust the decision reached. When paired with the King of Swords, this card indicates a legal matter or court decision. The level of success in this issue may be revealed by the surrounding cards.

The shadowy forest shows that nature also has a hand in justice, for while there is law, there is also the law of returns, karma, and retribution achieved by the actions of others who carry out the decision and return the scales to balance. The small grassy clearing is sprinkled with daisies, for truth, authority, harmony, and communication, while a spider, a symbol of power, wisdom, and balance, weaves a web between two of the circle stones.

Meaning: Objectivity, impartiality, trust your own decision, fairness, balance, truth, virtue, honor, law, prevail in a legal matter, equilibrium, an agent working on your behalf, advice, consideration, conscience, impartiality, equity, reward, verdict, retribution for the aggrieved, harmony, natural law.

Reversed: Misrepresentation, bias, intolerance, legal action delayed, complications, gossip, false accusation, tedious bureaucracy, cloudy perception.

Prompt Words: Objectivity, fairness, trust your own decision.

*Notes:*_____

_____

_____

_____

_____

_____

_____

_____

_____

_____

_____

_____

_____

_____

_____

_____

_____

_____

_____

_____

_____

_____

_____

_____

_____

_____

_____

12–The Oak King

The Oak King hangs upside down by his heel, which is wedged between branches in an oak tree. He is comfortable, casual, and relaxed as he contemplates his vital role within the infinite passage of time, tracing on the ground below him the perpetual cosmic lemniscate within the circle of the year. His position reflects the infinity symbol as he anticipates the familiar cycle of change, when the Oak King transitions into the unborn infant within the womb of the Earth Mother, surrendering his reign to himself as Holly King, the Sage who will rule until the Oak King is reborn at Yule. The lemniscate shows that the God's endless cycle of life and authority is a harmonious interaction of light and shadow, demonstrating that life itself moves through seasons of its own, and he is the guide.

This card offers the opportunity to meditate or focus inward and determine what needs to be released to make room for what needs to be brought in, and what needs to be retained. This can be an external or internal housecleaning, deciding what is unnecessary in one's life, what is worthy of being kept, and what will be new and beneficial. Here is a time when the conscious and subconscious may communicate, discovering what is desired and what is no longer necessary in one's life.

The matter of change is in the tenuous phase of transition, requiring thought and the willingness to let go of the outmoded in order to reach achievement in some area of life. This is the stage of determining what foundation will be laid for the future and what new venture or outlook should begin. When this card appears in a reading, one is advised to take the time to consider the various options, pull together resources, and bring everything into balance before proceeding. Just as spell materials are set on a pentacle during magical work for grounding and manifestation in the physical world, so too should one prepare for what will materialize.

Yellow gorse, for hope, endurance, fertility, and rebirth, grows near the base of the tree. On a sunlit branch, a robin, signifying change, awareness of cycles, and messages, sits watching.

Meaning: Paused activity, transition, meditation, weighing options, inner peace, patience, deciding what changes to make, self-sacrifices for gains.

Reversed: Decision made, time for action, missed opportunity, fear of change.

Prompt Words: Introspection, inner peace.

*Notes:*_____
_____
_____
_____
_____
_____
_____
_____
_____
_____
_____
_____
_____
_____
_____
_____
_____
_____
_____
_____
_____
_____
_____
_____
_____
_____
_____

13–The Lord of Shadows

This is a card of change, moving from shadow into light. Some things that have hampered this change are put aside to make the transition possible. The God of Nature in his aspect of Lord of Shadows, ruler of the underworld, pauses in the shadows of the forest to watch an elderly man with his grandson walk away from a well with a full bucket of water. In early times the well was a metaphor of life-force energy, the magical waters of life that sustained one's creative spirit and joy of being. The man and child show the generations that flow from the water of life, the satisfaction of a life well lived under the bright light of the Sun.

The Lord of Shadows, with an air of patience and kindness, holds in his hand a twig of yew. His presence suggests a life in transition, with the obstacles to transformation being cleared away. There needs to be a clean sweep for the right changes to come to fruition, for only in this way is there progress and improvement. Sometimes this comes as a matter of course in one's life. Refusal to accept a new outlook may engender a loss of hope, stagnation, or a lack of growth. It is from the cleansing that new optimism arises, removing negative influences and allowing positive ones to enter. Old situations give way to new ones, and the past is left behind as a person moves on, released from prior commitments.

As with Samhain, when the veil between the worlds is thinnest and all worlds are linked in hallows, there is a quiet knowing with this card that cleansing is taking place in one's life and there is an opportunity to commune with the inner self. From this comes the insight needed to release negativity and take steps toward a positive change and new direction.

The yew tree, with its red berries, represents the underworld, change, rebirth, and renewal. A luna moth, for transitions and moving toward the light, flies gracefully from the shadows toward the sunlit countryside.

Meaning: Change, moving from shadow into light, finding new meaning in life, a turning point in life, optimism, removal of obstructions, creating positive changes, new outlook and actions replace the outmoded.

Reversed: Stagnation, immobility, resistance to change, self-evaluation needed.

Prompt Words: Change, transformation, turning point for improvement.

*Notes:*_____

_____

_____

_____

_____

_____

_____

_____

_____

_____

_____

_____

_____

_____

_____

_____

_____

_____

_____

_____

_____

_____

_____

_____

_____

_____

14–The Sidhe

This is a card of balance and flow between two worlds and consciousness. Here the Witch listens to the whispers of the Sidhe, the faerie folk who help her to concoct a potion that will be exactly right for her purpose. The power of this image lies in the transforming action of the spirits and entities of nature working with someone who is able to harmonize the rational mind with the intuitive mind, the solar energy with the lunar energy. The interaction between reality and idealism invigorates both and brings about the balance between the physical and psychic realms necessary for magical works.

When this card appears in a reading, there is a message of good people skills and the ability to communicate with others so they are willing to help one accomplish a task. In the physical world, this manifests as someone who is a good organizer and knows how to present ideas in a way that generates enthusiasm and support from coworkers, superiors, and peers. This card can also indicate improvement in one's health, or new enthusiasm for work or objectives.

The Sidhe bring the inspiration of new ideas into the mind of the person who assimilates them and brings thought into reality through the assistance of others. In the spiritual realm, new awareness and insights are brought to the individual to be shared with other people.

Patience is indicated, for the information or idea has to be brought to others in terms they can understand. Changes may have to be made to accommodate and meld the idea into reality, but this is handled with confidence and an eye to the outcome, the bigger picture. Through fusion and compromise, teamwork and harmony of purpose ensue and the vision comes to life in the material world. Moderation rather than forcefulness gets the job done.

A bundle of lavender, for faerie aid, magic, clarity, and harmony, is in the vase on the table. In the moonlight through the open window can be seen a cow, a symbol for Goddess connection, ever present in the life of the Witch, bringing enlightenment and nurturing the spirit.

Meaning: Inspiration, patience, temperance, fusion, invigoration, blending ideas, harmony of the rational and the intuitive, consolidation to overcome differences, reconciliation, infusion of power, diplomacy, trusting intuition, skill in the arts.

Reversed: Discord, uncompromising, imbalance, competitiveness, impatience, frustration.

Prompt Words: Harmony, good people skills.

*Notes:*_____

_____

_____

_____

_____

_____

_____

_____

_____

_____

_____

_____

_____

_____

_____

_____

_____

_____

_____

_____

_____

_____

_____

_____

_____

15–Nature

This is the card of wild Nature, where the path chosen may be joyful and unrestricted or fraught with unseen dangers and overgrown vines. Here the trapper is setting a bear trap, unaware that a bear is behind him, watching. The man is equally oblivious to the fauns of the wilderness dancing in a distant clearing, one even beckoning to the bear.

Choices are the highlight of this card, as are possible repercussions. The warning is that short-term goals that require personal sacrifice are not always in one's best interests. Will the bear join in the revelry of the nature spirits, or will it risk being entrapped by reaching into something unnatural? People also choose the direction they travel in their lives, and sometimes what originally seems like a blessing turns out to be false. Then the choice becomes whether or not to liberate oneself. Staying in a job that pays well but has an unpleasant work environment or staying in an unrewarding relationship because of the expectations of others are only two examples of how one may take on undesired burdens. The restrictions that are self-imposed may also be self-released, so that one may better savor the joy of life and dance with the fauns. One may choose to act freely, to laugh at the result if necessary, or to be tied to a situation, a way of life, or an attitude that is not enjoyed or liked.

Following natural desire and inclination to find satisfaction in life is a matter of conscious deliberation and decision, whether in areas of attitude, materialism, or spirituality. Yet there is the allure of trying to control the material world or letting desires rule a person. The Divine in nature offers harmony in living a natural life, enjoying the material aspects as well as the spiritual, and regaining control over one's life and laughing at the tripping vines. This comfortable relationship with nature is part of the path of the Craft, allowing one to be linked with nature and the Divine.

Comfrey, symbolizing binding, control, and liberation from control, grows close to the trap. The black bear represents endurance, introspection, and decisions.

Meaning: Accept or release self-imposed restrictions, follow inclinations, potential is obstructed or unleashed, allow the natural course to flow, freedom, choose what appeals.

Reversed: Fear of change, inhibited, discontent, self-inflicted unhappiness.

Prompt Words: Choice of restriction or freedom.

*Notes:*_____

_____

_____

_____

_____

_____

_____

_____

_____

_____

_____

_____

_____

_____

_____

_____

_____

_____

_____

_____

_____

_____

_____

_____

_____

16–The Wild Hunt

The Wild Hunt, lead by the God in his aspect of Hunter, is the turbulent Rade (ride) that travels in the night sky as severe winds, thunderous rolling black clouds, and streaks of jagged lightning. Their shocking passage initiates abrupt changes as they gather what is no longer viable along their route to the underworld. Here is liberation coming as an unstoppable but quickly passing storm, freeing the mind and invigorating the spirit as restrictions are blasted away. Bright light erupts through the confining tower top and shines as a beacon from the window as an expression of sudden enlightenment leading to new beginnings and new possibilities. This powerful energy in a reading offers the opportunity to cast off burdensome encumbrances that restrict a full life or the achievement of personal fulfillment. Mental and emotional stone towers that were constructed for protection from what has been feared block growth and potential, so the Wild Hunt opens the way for beneficial change and self-illumination. With the resulting awareness, hope is renewed, for whatever caused the initial surprise will pass. Instead, this is the opening necessary for self-improvement and a new outlook.

Insight abruptly revealed brings to light obstacles, misconceptions, and previously hidden truths requiring action. Change is in the air, and the universe is shoving the reluctant individual into removing the blinders, rejecting denial, and finally taking the long-overdue action for personal progress and spiritual growth. By overcoming the restraints previously self-imposed, internally or externally, fear evaporates and evolution can take place. Liberation from the same old routine, wrong job, false impressions, mistaken emotional connections, or delusions releases one from the trap of unhappiness and discontent. A person is set back on the right track, with peace and clarity coming as bright daybreak after a stormy night.

Patches of rue, for protection, destruction of negativity, release, and freedom, grow at the base by the tower door as a reminder that one is protected in this period of change. A crowing rooster, for awakening, courage, and daybreak, takes flight, just as one's spirit will be released from the darkness that held it in check.

Meaning: Sudden change, illumination, truth revealed, shocking event, end of illusions, enlightenment, unexpected events, enemies revealed, disruptions force change, deceit revealed, release from oppression, time to rebuild, negative situation ends.

Reversed: Resistance to change, ignoring reality, self-deception.

Prompt Words: Sudden change, shocking event.

*Notes:*_____

_____

_____

_____

_____

_____

_____

_____

_____

_____

_____

_____

_____

_____

_____

_____

_____

_____

_____

_____

_____

_____

_____

_____

_____

17–The Star

The card of the lucky Star shows there is energy abounding for a fortuitous opportunity to arrive through which one's hopes and dreams can be manifested. The seven-pointed Fairy Star represents the harmony of Land, Water, Sky, Moon, Sun, Stars, and Magic. Beneath the Star, the Goddess is revealed in her aspect of Faerie Queen, pouring out the waters of life to invigorate and encourage positive changes. She opens the way and offers the chance for a joyful transformation in one's life, yet leaves it up to the individual to take advantage of this. The card indicates that the prospects are excellent for making a change in one's life, moving in the direction one has desired but has not yet attained.

Whether one chooses to take advantage of the opportunity can be influenced by the other cards in the reading that may offer helpful clarification. The waters spilled from silver urns into the river and into a gazing bowl for divination suggest that one can gauge the future impact of taking up the opportunity. The Queen stands in the river, indicating that some solutions to problems reside in the subconscious mind. The Star implies that planetary or universal energies are in a favorable alignment at the time of the reading, and the addition of faerie influence provides an aspect of wishes granted through the blessings of devas and otherworld entities.

There is optimism and hope in this card, which is always an omen of good fortune and bringing desires into reality. The universe will provide the opening to push matters in a favorable direction for accomplishing what is most sought. The energy is gathered in one's favor and is ready to be utilized to carry out a goal.

Action should not be delayed any longer than necessary when the opportunity presents itself, for there is no indication of when this will happen again. Trust in the universe, the Divine, and one's own intuition is suggested. Saint John's wort, for faeries, magic, luck, and power, grows along the riverbank. A goldfish, a symbol of opportunities and balance, leaps joyfully out of the invigorating waters.

Meaning: An opportunity to manifest hopes and dreams, inspiration, creativity, talent recognized, positive energy, unexpected help, new ideas, gain a wish, positive future, bright prospects, chance to start over.

Reversed: Disappointment, doubts, distrust, insecurity, letting opportunities pass.

Prompt Words: Opportunity, hopes obtainable.

*Notes:*_____

_____

_____

_____

_____

_____

_____

_____

_____

_____

_____

_____

_____

_____

_____

_____

_____

_____

_____

_____

_____

_____

_____

_____

_____

_____

18–The Moon

This card shows that trusting one's instincts can be beneficial and prompts one to look beneath the surface of things before making a commitment of any kind, be it in work, career, purchases, or relationships. The reflection of the Full Moon on the water can indicate delusions, where it is easier or more attractive to believe an image rather than looking up at the Moon itself to know the reality. The hidden meanings of subconscious images or sensations can be translated for comprehension in the conscious mind. There could be dishonesty, deception, or insincerity around a person, so if they feel a nagging sensation that something is amiss in a matter, this deserves to be investigated.

Psychic awareness, dreams, and visions may also be factors when this card appears in a reading. The country Witch is going to the pond when the Moon is in this phase to work her magic rites and to honor the Goddess in her lunar aspect. This is a time for creating blessed water for spells and cleansings, walking between the worlds while remaining grounded, and utilizing psychic gifts for divination. The cauldron can be used to transform energy from visualization into physical presence, but with the caution of being certain what result is sought and not exploiting or deceiving others. The rule of "harm none" always applies.

The Full Moon is the phase of manifestation, with powerful energy to effect change, just as the Moon affects the tides of the earth and the fluids of one's own body, and thus is a perfect time for magical works with quick results. The pond is surrounded by hazelnut trees, alluding to the connection between Witches and faeries, particularly when working magic with the energies of nature.

Chamomile, for calm, intuition, and insight, grows along the path to the pool. A trout, a symbol of instinct, arcane wisdom, and divination, leaps from the water with a hazelnut of arcane wisdom in its mouth, brought to the surface from the bottom of the pond.

Meaning: Heed instincts, follow intuition, manifesting the subconscious, psychic vision or dreams, learning magic, exposing deception, look beyond the surface for hidden truths, unseen forces at work, cycles, intentions obscured, magical work with quick results, journeys, occult interests.

Reversed: Facades, delusions, manipulating others, suspicion, illusion, impractical ideas.

Prompt Words: Trust instincts.

*Notes:*_____

_____

_____

_____

_____

_____

_____

_____

_____

_____

_____

_____

_____

_____

_____

_____

_____

_____

_____

_____

_____

_____

_____

_____

_____

_____

19–The Sun

This is a card of achievement, security, and happiness. There is joy in an accomplishment that results in material and physical well-being. The light of the Sun energizes and showers prosperity and contentment, its life-giving power increasing joy and ensuring success. However, this is not a card of easy or unearned wealth and happiness, but one of satisfaction from a job well done. Even in reverse interpretations, the power of the Sun comes through, so that while it may mean an overabundance of optimism, it also shows that with more effort, aims may be achieved. The benefits of the Sun come from hard work and relate to the effort one puts into bringing about the desired results.

Self-expression in any field, from fine arts to scientific exploration, is also encouraged and linked to achievement. From this comes growing self-assurance, and the card may indicate honors or promotion in one's area of work or as objectives being attained.

The golden fields of ripening grain demonstrate the result of hard work well done, providing one with a sense of pride and satisfaction. The cozy cottage shows contentment, harmony, and comfort. The solar energy of the God fills the grain and likewise fills one's life with spiritual fulfillment, while the Goddess as the Earth Mother prepares for the first harvest, that of the grain at Lughnassadh, initiating the start of the harvest season that continues into early and late autumn. Even in modern times, harvest is a community matter, followed by fairs and contests of skill and strength. Thus this card also indicates that friendship and working in concert with others brings success, love, joy, happiness, and abundance.

A truly auspicious card in a reading, the Sun can also indicate marriage, depending on the other cards in the spread, such as the Two of Chalices, Three of Chalices, and Four of Wands, or it can indicate pregnancy if combined with the Earth Mother, Ace of Chalices, or Three of Chalices.

Sunflowers, signifying happiness, joy, well-being, and harmony, grow in glorious profusion beside the cottage. A golden eagle, symbolizing success and achievement, soars above the cottage in the bright sunlit sky.

Meaning: Success, achievement, happiness, joy, good health, children, material well-being, satisfaction from efforts, optimism, harmony, recognition, individuality, creativity, accomplishment, new cycle beginning, community, friendship, contentment, marriage, pregnancy.

Reversed: Delay, temporary setback, overextended, overly optimistic, isolation, lack of effort.

Prompt Words: Happiness, achievement.

*Notes:*_____
_____
_____
_____
_____
_____
_____
_____
_____
_____
_____
_____
_____
_____
_____
_____
_____
_____
_____
_____
_____
_____
_____
_____

20–Harvest

This card symbolizes reaping rewards from what has been sown, bringing forth a rebirth and a sense of renewal. Here the farmer has been working closely with nature, as evidenced by the presence of helpful brownies. The family has brought in their abundance and now may enjoy the fruits of their labors. The jug and mug of spirits symbolize the second harvest, that of fruit and vine at Mabon, when the God invests his spirit into the beverages as he departs to reign in the underworld until Yule. The table is laden with the bounty of nature through the blessings of the Divine. Grains, vegetables, fruit, jugs of wine, mead, and beer are the products of a season of nurturing and careful tending and pruning to reap good rewards. Fresh game birds hang by the cottage door, showing that the cycles of nature are always in motion and one season's harvest segues into that of the next. This card indicates that one is ready to gather in the harvest of past efforts, and a transformation is taking place with the infusion of life essence.

With a sense of revelation and insight comes renewed energy, but also a time of accountability or reckoning resulting from actions taken, choices made, and opportunities ignored. There may be a need for self-assessment as to whether one's decisions have been beneficial or detrimental to personal growth and spiritual peace. Some form of atonement for past actions may be initiated or forced upon oneself through the judgments of others. Along with this evaluation is the potential for a rebirth, with new insight as to direction or possible changes in one's life, and even an influx of psychic awareness and understanding through an altered state as the second harvest is celebrated with the wine of life. With revelation and insight comes renewed energy for further transformative action.

Garden fennels, for blessings, energy, protection, and security, grow in a large container box in front of the house, while a goat, a symbol for abundance, rebirth, renewal, and vitality, nibbles the grass nearby.

Meaning: Reaping a good harvest, efforts rewarded, accountability, renewal, potential fulfilled, revitalization, good health restored, rebirth, self-evaluation, making a major decision, need for discretion, a conflict concludes favorably, a new awakening, judgment, atonement, making changes for the better.

Reversed: Hesitancy, indecision, disappointing returns for efforts, correcting past mistakes, working toward improvement.

Prompt Words: Rewards, renewal.

*Notes:*_____

_____

_____

_____

_____

_____

_____

_____

_____

_____

_____

_____

_____

_____

_____

_____

_____

_____

_____

_____

_____

_____

_____

_____

_____

_____

21–The World Tree

In this card, the elementals, in their relation to the changing of the seasons, are reflected through the branches of the World Tree. The snake of wisdom, sometimes considered to be a beautiful serpent or a dragon, lies at the roots of the tree, for wisdom is the foundation of growth. The branches of this tree reside in the midst of the universe, equally balanced by Sun and Moon, God and Goddess, with its roots transiting the shadowy realms below, ruled by the Divine in their aspects of Hunter and Crone, Lord of Shadows and Lady of Wisdom. The image reflects the formula of "as above, so below," with the image of the tree distilling the cosmic cycles with those of the earth and the individual. This card reflects the celebration and joy of achievement and of a successfully concluded effort, yet the card acknowledges that this ending is actually the prelude to a fresh start. The World Tree of good conclusions and joyful new beginnings leads to the Greenman as the cycle is resumed.

There may be the attainment of objectives, or honors and material gains that lead to greater responsibilities, but with this comes a quickening that hints at more lying just beneath the surface. The motion of the cosmos is evident, and the cycles of life and the substrata of the moments of life are recognized as merely markers on the soul's journey in the physical, spiritual, mental, or emotional planes. It is the end of one era and the beginning of another, good conclusions and joyful new beginnings. This card is one of hope and optimism in the face of inevitable change, for change is part of life.

A large ash tree, representing stability, connections, astral realms, spirits, and magical strength, is traditionally seen as the World Tree. The graceful serpent, a symbol of wisdom, cycles, and regeneration, weaves its way through the roots of the tree. A white crane flies by the tree and represents cycles, transformation, and the union of the otherworld, middleworld, and underworld.

Meaning: Wholeness, objectives attained, good conclusions, end of a matter, time for something new, completion, success, joy, advancement, achievement, fulfillment, recognition, all is in balance, transition, honors, perfection, reassurance.

Reversed: Unfinished work or project, unresolved situation, success brings new burdens, seeking attainment, payback, stagnation of efforts, more work needed.

Prompt Words: Completion, wholeness.

*Notes:*_____

_____

_____

_____

_____

_____

_____

_____

_____

_____

_____

_____

_____

_____

_____

_____

_____

_____

_____

_____

_____

_____

_____

_____

_____

_____

Chapter Two

The Minor Arcana

Pentacles

EARTH

material • physical • money
business • comfort • health
north • winter

Ace of Pentacles

This is a card of prosperity in the material world. It can indicate huge commercial success, strong business sense, financial success, rewards, and monetary gains. It can also represent physical well-being, good health, a secure income, and contentment. The green tones in the image reflect the energy of earthly wealth. This is the card of material goods, business ability, and fruits of labor realized. The oak pentacle is a symbol of manifestation and the earth elemental, and the ace is a power card showing accomplishment and positive results in matters of finance, business, construction, health, and secure income. This card may also indicate a new job, promotion, or pay raise, which may be clarified by the other cards in the spread. An auspicious card of good fortune and bliss, the Ace of Pentacles shows worthwhile efforts and productivity that pay off, as well as spiritual well-being.

Warmed by the radiant sun, the manor house and lands present an image of comfort and satisfaction in the material world. As the elemental power of earth, the Ace of Pentacles represents the winter months of December, January, and February for the purpose of timing in relation to other cards in a reading. Cinquefoil, an herb of prosperity, wealth, and success, wraps around the pentacle. Sheep, symbols of abundance, well-being, generosity, and wealth, graze contentedly.

Meaning: Prosperity, material achievement, financial power, earnings, growth, sound business sense, commercial success, favorable period of financial security, attainment, well-being, new money venture, good financial news, business or financial opportunity, growth, promotion, pay raise, acquisition of material goods, good use of resources, productivity, contentment.

Reversed: Opportunity not fully realized, financial stagnation, disappointing financial gains, discomfort, physical limitations, lack of growth or gains, miserly.

Prompt Words: Prosperity, commercial success.

Two of Pentacles

This card shows a farmer balancing two pentacles, indicating his ability to balance finances as well as learn new skills, as progress in his area of expertise creates changes in methods. As a card of practicing dexterity, this card indicates energy being directed with determination to accomplish something for job, financial, or personal security. New approaches at work or a promotion could require specialized training, but the person has the ability to pick up these new skills with ease. While others may struggle or resist change, this person moves with confidence, adapting easily to new situations and requirements. The farmer depicted is unconcerned about the coming storm, for he knows his job and has secured his barn, so he is prepared for anything.

In some cases this card indicates balancing two jobs for financial security, but with the resolve necessary to carry on until finances improve. It could also be a card of apprenticeship, learning from a master or other professional, or it could simply show the need to live within a budget, depending on surrounding cards.

Patchouli, an herb of growth, knowledge, and balancing finances, grows by the barn. A fox, for adaptability, cleverness, determination, and agility, walks nearby.

Meaning: Balancing finances, learning new skills, agile with finances, energy for attaining goals, next phase in work begins, employment opportunity, learning stage passes quickly, weighing work choices or options for a business decision.

Reversed: Difficult situation requires careful balance, need to live within means, lack of enthusiasm for changes needed for success, stress.

Prompt Words: Balancing finances, learning new skills.

Three of Pentacles

This is the card of the craftsman who has learned a trade and secured the approval of his mentors, peers, and potential employers. Here the young bard has completed training and receives his harp, readying him for making a living in a professional capacity. This card may indicate a graduation from a school, university, apprenticeship, or technical training. The person is taking the step from an instructional environment and successfully putting the knowledge and skills learned to work. Contracts and official papers are possibilities, either as proof of successful completion of training or for employment, license, or some other requirement for working within a job field. As this is a card of individual ability, there could be a promotion, pay raise, or other suitable reward for work accomplished. One's talent, creativity, and personal worth is noted by higher-ups. The skill learned is a useful one, earning respect, prestige, and fair wages. A person may have gained strong patrons through developing skills during the learning process. Depending on other cards in the reading, a pregnancy could be indicated.

Reeds represent learning, concentration, focus, confidence, and talent. A heron, a symbol of learning, knowledge, opportunities, and skills, stands nearby.

Meaning: Celebrity from skills, apprenticeship pays off, contracts, skills, artistic talent, powerful support, rewards, renown, business opportunity, possible pregnancy.

Reversed: Indifference, lack of skills, refusing advice or training.

Prompt Words: Celebrity, work rewarded.

Four of Pentacles

This is a card of security concerns. A person is focused on security of home and finances, saving money yet also having money to spend. This card indicates a cautious approach to friendship and socializing—not antisocial, but just careful and perhaps a little suspicious of the motives of others. Access to the home is restricted until a person is more familiar with would-be guests. Such a person does not appreciate uninvited or unexpected visitors to the home, nor a presumption of personal familiarity. Reserved, careful, and self-contained, the person is possibly living in comfortable circumstances but has concerns about being taken advantage of and losing what has been gained. Financial security is of paramount importance, and this state is well entrenched. What is earned is kept in reserve, perhaps building up a savings account or being directed into a fund. This is the card of a private person, one who may be influential but also selective of associates. There may be a financial blockage or simply an unwillingness to spend money. This is a thrifty person, so gift-giving is likely limited by price.

Nettle, an herb of security, home protection, and increasing finances, is kept by the door of the house. A turtle, a symbol of security, abundance, defense, and relationships, withdraws into his shell.

Meaning: Security of home and finances, careful spending, saving money, budgeting, controlling personal access, feeling insecure, blocked expression, social reluctance, reserved nature, socially shy, suspicious of others' motives, selective of associates, a small gift, endurance, pay raise, increase in income, income directed to private enjoyment of beauty.

Reversed: Extravagance, greed, coming into a legacy, gains from a loss, delays, miserly, materialistic.

Prompt Words: Financial security, self-contained, withdrawn.

Five of Pentacles

Although one of the elements of this card is poverty in the presence of plenty, it is also a card of self-imposed isolation. Despite the golden pentacles on the barren branches of the poplar tree, the woman's focus is on her empty purse. The implication of being left out in the cold is countered by the warm light from the stone circle. Things hidden will soon become evident, and the sense of isolation and tight funds is only a temporary condition. There could be unexpected expenses coming, so be prepared to have money set aside for emergencies.

This card may appear when someone has been passed over for a promotion or pay raise, or when one has moved to an unfamiliar location and has yet to get one's bearings and make new friends. Things may be difficult at present or money may be tight, but change is coming, so patience is needed. A person is advised by this card to be careful with money and not to give loans to people who may not pay them back on time or at all, and not to give extravagant gifts to unappreciative people.

The poplar tree symbolizes problems, loss, and defense of money. A lizard, representing fears and loss, lodges in the tree.

Meaning: Unexpected expenses, financial worries, overextended, temporary material instability, feeling isolated, dissatisfaction with the status quo, busywork, negative trend will be reversed in time.

Reversed: Troubles overcome, relief comes, courage to find hidden opportunities.

Prompt Words: Financial worries, unexpected expenses.

Six of Pentacles

This is a card of generosity, with care being taken to ensure the recipient is worthy of the gift. While this can indicate sharing one's personal abundance, it is also a card of pay raises, bonuses, and promotion, especially with the Six of Wands, Ace of Pentacles, or the Battle Wagon. The giver of this generosity must determine what is the right amount and who is the right person to receive the money. This card can also represent giving a portion of one's income to charity or charitable institutions, possibly by allotment or tithe. There may be a small gift for a special occasion such as a graduation or birthday. Depending on the other cards in a spread, the querent may be either the giver or the recipient of someone else's kindness. This card shows that no matter what a person's financial station in life, there are always those who could benefit from an act of simple kindness in hard times. In some cases it could indicate one is supporting others through one's prosperity, or there may be charity work involved.

Meadowsweet, for favors, power, and balance, is offered by the vendor. A woodpecker, for generosity, cycles, and growth, watches from a tree.

Meaning: Generosity, donation, bonus, rewards, promotion, gifts, gratification, material increase, sharing bounty, beneficiary of another's bounty, self-confidence, gains from extra effort.

Reversed: Debts, greed, materialism, overspending, envy, loss through negligence or theft, money owed to others.

Prompt Words: Generosity, rewards.

Seven of Pentacles

This card shows that progress is being made on a long-term project, but there is much work yet to be done. There is no time to stop and play, but sticking with the job will see it through to completion and then the rewards can be reaped. There is a warning of impatience here that suggests shortcuts might be considered but are not appropriate for the project and could potentially ruin the effort. Decisions need to be made as the work progresses, changing some things that are not working out and smoothing out the rough edges of the project.

As the project nears completion, there is a tendency to want to rush and get the job done or to abandon the effort. If rushed, the work could be sloppy and unacceptable, wasting previous labor. Although the fruits of that labor are nearing completion, the harvest cannot be rushed, so patience is still needed to see the project through. This card could appear when someone has put a lot of effort into something and is feeling exhausted and ready to quit just short of completing the task. Other cards may offer encouragement to persevere or may support abandoning the work.

Skullcap, for focus, creativity, and overcoming stress, grows in a planter. A kite (bird), a symbol of concentration, skills, and motivation, swoops in the sky close by.

Meaning: Long-term work project, productivity, business start, work decision needs careful consideration, progress, nurturing a project or plan, impatient for rewards, goals achieved in due time, hard work will pay off, focus on labors.

Reversed: Goals achieved, minimal rewards, imprudent action, unwillingness to work toward a goal.

Prompt Words: Nurturing a long-term project.

Eight of Pentacles

This card shows that a person enjoys the work being done and is looking at the long-term value of having a career, with retirement, benefits, and a pension. Utilizing one's skills and talents ensures one's work never becomes old or boring, because each day brings the pleasure of doing a job that is understood and secure. Craftsmanship may be indicated, but the card can apply to any line of work, indicating the intention of reaping the rewards of a full career. Having persevered through a training program, internship, or apprenticeship, the person goes on to blend skill and productivity. There is a degree of pride and growing confidence over the years of work, but also a continuing attention to detail coupled with the ability to make prudent work decisions along the way. The vocation has commercial value and the individual is able to profit from skill and training. A promotion, pay raise, or bonus may be coming, depending on the influence of other cards in the reading. Overall, the desire is for a successful endeavor with a future reward for years of service. This card may relate to creating and vending handicrafts at a local level (such as at fairs or flea markets), creating products for catalogs and mass market sales, or designing components for industry. Personal skills are capitalized upon for commercial gain, with an eye toward at being comfortable in old age.

Lilacs, for business, security, creativity, and focus, grow by the door. A pigeon, a symbol of security, home, and luck, is nearby.

Meaning: Enjoying one's work, a career with benefits and retirement, expertise is rewarded, promotion, satisfying work, skills and talent applied toward commercial gains, individuality is appreciated, developing lifelong hobbies or skills.

Reversed: Short-term vision in work, minimal rewards, wasted effort, poor investment, job dissatisfaction.

Prompt Words: Commercial skills, work enjoyment.

Nine of Pentacles

This card shows contentment and satisfaction with one's life and efforts. It indicates good self-esteem from knowing one's value and worth. There is no question of ability, but instead an awareness of one's ability to make a good living. A comfortable life may be the result of education that leads to better work opportunities, or it may the result of some unexpected good fortune. There is gain in all areas of life, a congenial lifestyle, and accomplishment. Security is assured, but there may also be a surprise gift or money arriving as well.

Along with the sense of well-being is an indication of refinement and prudence, perhaps even healing ability. A prudent use of talent, skills, and finances allows for a congenial home life and sense of self-sufficiency. The quiet confidence and warm emotions emanating through this scene of a family at ease emphasize the comfort derived from a realistic appreciation of one's own skills and taking pleasure in the rewards thereof. There is time for the individual to relax and enjoy the good things in life.

Sage, an herb of business, comfort, prosperity, and harmony, grows in a large pot. A salamander, a symbol of comfort, connections, and manifesting goals, crawls along the woodpile.

Meaning: Good self-esteem, accomplishment, financial security, well-being, sudden good luck, money from unexpected sources, a comfortable home, discernment, growth, prudence, discretion, love of nature, a gift coming.

Reversed: Discontent, insecurity, imprudence, fear of loss, self-deprecating, financial embarrassment, health issues, loss of valued possessions, unconfident.

Prompt Words: Self-esteem, comfort.

Ten of Pentacles

This is a card of prosperity that leads to happiness with home and family. The supportive family environment offers emotional and financial security. As an undertone in this card, there is heritage in the sense of family continuity that may be manifested as money or goods passed along through the generations, as with heirlooms, traditions, or stories. This card also indicates accumulated wealth bringing stability and ongoing contentment to the family. The timing of this prosperity may be in middle life rather than something one is born into, showing that finances have been carefully handled to ensure future security and provide for the needs of the family, perhaps as investments or savings for the education or vocational training for the children.

Another aspect of this card is that of buying or selling a house or property, refinancing the property, or spending money on redecorating or making repairs. It can also imply an extended family dwelling together, perhaps three generations under one roof, or a family providing for the care of family members. Depending on the surrounding cards, this card could indicate a change of location, such as selling one house and buying another. While it is generally an auspicious card, there may be other issues concerning possession of the home if there are other cards in the spread that relate to legal matters or inheritances.

Cowslip, for prosperity, beauty, and protection, grows along the garden wall. A kingfisher, a symbol of prosperity, harmony, and happiness, is perched on a branch, gazing into the pond.

Meaning: Prosperity for the home, buying, selling, redecorating, refinancing, making home repairs, favorable placement, good investments, fruitful marriage, stability, legacy, family heritage, heirlooms, traditions being passed to the next generation, contentment, supportive family environment.

Reversed: Disruptions, family quarrels, problems with a legacy, loss of inheritance, gambling.

Prompt Words: Prosperity for the home.

Page of Pentacles

This is the card of the student, one who studies in a practical field from which a living can be earned. The emphasis is on taking an interest and developing it into a career that makes the effort worthwhile. The child here has made his own magical tool, the pentacle, and is practicing consecrating it through transferring energy with his hand. The card shows the ability to turn an interest into a profitable career through diligent application of energy and effort. The power of youthful enthusiasm and vision adds energy to the new project and could indicate that a new identity or lifestyle is being assumed. There is potential for financial independence brought about by developing new talents and skills, so it is also a card of initial scholarship or educational studies. As this is a card of the student, there could be associated financing involved, possibly clarified through other cards in the reading. The card could relate to one's children or to studies undertaken and the application of what has been learned.

Sprigs of vervain, an herb of beginnings, consecration, protection, and children, are tied and hung near a window to dry. A Corgi dog, representing faeries and guardianship, jumps up with excitement at the boy's achievement.

Meaning: Practical studies, using interests to generate income, practicing learned skills, studious, news about lifestyle, personal identity, diligence, scholarship, business deals, practical developing skills, seeking more responsibility, higher education, completing studies for future gains.

Reversed: Unrealistic goals, excessive vanity, unwilling to work toward goals, dissatisfaction with work or career choice, need for more study, impulsive false start.

Prompt Words: Practical studies, diligence in studies.

Knight of Pentacles

This is the card of a new career adventure and an auspicious occasion. There is energy and enthusiasm for the new project or new job. There may be some kind of progression in training involved, as with levels of skilled craftsmanship from apprentice to master. The indication is that there is an auspicious change on the horizon, something sought and approached with unbounded eagerness. The card could refer to a new project, a new job, or even entry into military service where one may learn a skill or trade.

Here the Knight of Pentacles is a young woman. Leaving the farm and freshly plowed fields behind her, she rides her muscular workhorse and carries her earned pay in a pouch on her belt. She is excited and determined to make her way in the wider world, earning a living through her hard work, for with her draft horse she can hire out to plow fields at different farms. This card indicates a useful person who offers stability and approaches work in a reliable and methodical manner, yet is able to implement new ideas and carry them through to a satisfactory conclusion.

Peonies, flowers for business and opportunities, are carried by the Knight of Pentacles. A falcon, a symbol of loyalty, security, and communication, flies near the knight.

Meaning: Job opportunity, auspicious occasion, useful person, responsible and competent worker, new career adventure, enthusiasm, reliable worker, goals achieved, beginning of a new stage of work or career, diligent service, consistent effort applied to tasks, gentle and methodical, good business sense, self-reliant.

Reversed: Recklessness, complacent, idle, incompetence.

Prompt Words: Job opportunity, new career adventure.

Queen of Pentacles

This card indicates that financial plans are coming together. There is a sense of peace and tranquility fostered by financial security and plans set favorably in motion. Here the Queen of Pentacles sits comfortably in her fruitful pecan grove. Bountiful nature offers stability, and she feels the kindly influence of nature's energies working with her. When this card appears in a reading, one has the ability to bring to fruition plans leading to economic security and well-being. Nurturing practical ambitions brings self-sufficiency and confidence. One may be inclined to luxury and seeking social standing, but this is tempered by generosity.

This card suggests planning ahead and having those plans work out as hoped. Money resources are under control, so there is calm wisdom in money management and a strong, sensible utilization of funds. There is prosperity and independence as well. Sometimes this card may signify a single-parent household where finances are carefully monitored, or a lesser income that is successfully supplementing a larger one to have money for lighthearted entertainment, vacations, or small luxuries.

Pecans, for prosperity and abundance, are gathered in a basket beside the Queen of Pentacles. A white dove, a symbol of prosperity, harmony, and wisdom, sits on a tree branch.

Meaning: Financial plans realized, fruitfulness, independence, work rewarded, stability, dignity, practical ambitions, attainment of physical goals, self-sufficiency, able to provide for self and others, social position and success.

Reversed: Financial negligence, loose spending, self-indulgence, suspicious.

Prompt Words: Financial plans realized.

King of Pentacles

This card shows economic power and the ability to realize one's ambitions. There is a talent for business and a kindly interest in giving sound economic advice. Stability and success are possibly achieved through a lifetime of work or finding the field of one's highest aptitude to focus upon for commercial profit.

Personal creativity may be manifested through sound business sense, but there is also an inherent social responsibility. Here is someone who is willing to instruct others or give them advice so they can work toward their own economic goals. The King of Pentacles shows that good plans have been put to use with practical wisdom for strong economic gains. This card indicates a successful leader, perhaps a manager or corporate officer or self-employed entrepreneur who knows how to get things done while still being sensitive to the needs of employees. There is a strong sense of purpose in what is attempted, so that through a methodical approach, ideas are manifested. If adversely connected to other cards in a reading, this business leader could be more tyrannical than beneficial, more jealous of safeguarding business secrets than sharing wisdom.

High John, for business success, wealth, power, and support, grows on a trellis behind the King of Pentacles. A bull, a symbol of leadership, stability, and authority, calmly grazes in the pasture.

Meaning: Successful business leader, trustworthy business consultant, steadfast, generous, methodical, economic power, sensible financial planning, strong business sense, financial advice, real estate transactions, able to meet challenges.

Reversed: Materialism, greed, tyrannical, dullness, speculation, vicious old man, unable to bring ideas into reality, rigid attitudes.

Prompt Words: Economic power, helpful business leader.

Athames

AIR

mind • intellect • power
strength • conflict • worry
east • spring

Ace of Athames

This is a card of victory, and that energy can be applied in whatever area of life desired. There is strength of purpose for success in any field, and as it represents the power of elemental air, there is also the clarity of mind necessary to put that energy to work for achievement. The blue sky, white clouds, and light emphasize the power of the intellect to conceive ideas and work out solutions to problems. Triumph over obstacles is gained through the application of sound judgment and careful planning. The Ace of Athames shows that one has the mental agility to overcome obstacles and conflicts to accomplish an objective. The approach is one of assertive action to bring a problem or project to a satisfying conclusion. An aggressive attitude or quick mind demonstrates that one has the aptitude to handle and surmount any hurdle to achieving one's aspirations. If a health issue is concerned, this card may denote strength, a successful treatment, or perhaps a beneficial surgery. As the elemental power of air, the Ace of Athames represents the spring months of March, April, and May for the purpose of timing in relation to other cards in a reading.

Dandelions, herbs of power, skill, authority, and keen intellect, grow beneath the athame. A field mouse, a symbol of skills, success, and focus, clings to a stem and watches dandelion seeds take flight.

Meaning: Victory, success, achievement, strength, breakthrough, power to achieve goals, conquest, intellectual power, clarity of thought, mental agility, wisdom, strong will, great determination, enlightenment, truth, strength in health matters, surgery.

Reversed: Tyranny, self-destructive, obstacles, inaction, hindrance to plans, quick-tempered.

Prompt Words: Victory, strength.

Two of Athames

This is a card of negotiations. Here two fields need to be harvested and the men need to decide to cooperate and determine whose field will be first. There is an element of negotiation, give and take, and compromise with the Two of Athames. When this card shows up in a reading, there is much to gained by being flexible and willing to accept a little less than was desired in order to keep the peace and for the greater good. In business matters, one may have to negotiate a contract, accept a performance review with a smaller pay increase than desired for the good of the company, and so on. There is the possibility of calling a truce in arguments or blending elements of two ideas to create a new perspective. This card shows that a temporary reprieve in the form of negotiation will allow time for a more permanent arrangement to be made. There is a sense of tension underlying an appearance of tranquility, indicating a time for the delicate work of diplomacy while also suggesting that making an important decision may bring peace of mind.

Pennyroyal, an herb of inner calm, peace, and healing, grows around the base of the stump. A starling, a symbol of communication, strength, and peace, flies overhead.

Meaning: Uncomfortable truce, negotiation, compromise, keeping the peace for the greater good, balance of opposites, tension to maintain the peace, cool analysis in decisions, harmony of power, temporary solutions, tension below the surface, diplomacy, problem resolved, reconciliation, patience, overcoming present difficulties, tensions ease, vital decision.

Reversed: Duplicity, indecision, malice, false friends, efforts frustrated.

Prompt Words: Negotiations, compromise.

Three of Athames

This is a card that expresses the need to avoid agonizing over a decision. This decision is a matter of personal choice, so if it is something one desires to do, then one may proceed. If it is something not desired, then one may back away. The choice to proceed may be a leap of faith, and once it is made, one should not worry about the decision. Here the woman needs to decide if she will stay in this cottage, making repairs and cleaning it up to be a comfortable home, or if she should look elsewhere. Evaluating the possibilities may be part of making a decision, considering which elements are appealing and which are objectionable. But don't overthink the matter. Here the woman stands at the threshold to the unknown, but whether she stays or leaves, whether she takes that first step or not, is a matter of choice. There may be a sense of sorrow or loss involved, something that has led up to this decision time, but this should not cloud the person's ultimate decision of whether or not to proceed. At present, the way is uncertain, but once that first step is taken, the way becomes clear. This card may appear in readings for people who leave home for long periods of time or who are moving to a new location.

Mugwort, an herb of confidence, protection, and warding off negativity, grows alongside the pond. A swan, a symbol of transformation, change, quest, and manifestation, swims in the pond.

Meaning: Taking a new path to the unknown requires courage, unfinished business, absence, separation, resolving conflicts or problems thoughtfully, a new life, independence, transition, upheaval, discarding unnecessary fears for a leap of faith.

Reversed: Fear of loss, confusion, strife, discord, malice nearby.

Prompt Words: Agonizing over a decision.

Four of Athames

This is a card of respite from difficult activities. It could be a pause between major events or a vacation away from the commotion of the workplace routine. This is a time for replenishing energy and getting one's thoughts in order. Sometimes it is necessary to take a break to rest and let the mind sort out plans and create new ideas. The serenity offered here is accompanied by a readiness to resume action as needed. This can indicate taking a break from the cares and frustrations of life, or simply stepping back from a conflict for a moment to reassess the situation with composure rather than the heat of contention. There is an implied preparedness and a sense of being careful not to let one's guard down even when things seem to have calmed down. Applied to attitudes and perceptions, this card could suggest that one feels one's plans are under attack by others who are aggressively pushing for their own agendas. A heightened sense of competition may be more in the mind than in reality, so taking a time-out to reconsider matters is beneficial. There is also a possibility of needing time to recuperate from illness or injury.

Lily of the valley, a flower of calm, healing, and peace, grows near the river. A loon, a symbol of serenity, peace, and dream work, swims in the water.

Meaning: Vacation, recuperation, getting plans in order, patient but vigilant, tensions ease, gathering thoughts and strength in solitude, rest after a period of stress, recuperation from an illness, replenishment, temporary resolution of conflict, taking a break from the normal routine, relaxing, cleansing oneself of other people's energies, releasing burdens.

Reversed: Exclusion, paranoia, illness requires rest, careful renewal of activities, taking precautions, agitation, sleeplessness.

Prompt Words: Vacation, rest.

Five of Athames

This is a card that can be read from the perspective of the crafts-man or the merchant who is interested in buying the products. Ideas or plans of others are being collected for good use, and this may be viewed from the position of either the strong or the weak. There may be a conflict of ideas implied, or a struggle between the new and the entrenched. There may be a loss of pride, or self-esteem may suffer, but this can be overcome for later success. Here the craftsman is surrendering his work to one who is in a position to purchase it but has no regard for the skill that went into making it. Valid concepts and self-worth may face a challenge, but this may be a time of paying one's dues before confidence returns. Overcoming the anxiety of potential defeat is needed to bolster self-confidence and gain the respect and accord of opponents or competitors. Ideas and how others react to them, or defense of a higher principle, may be involved.

Geraniums, for concentration, self-confidence, and overcoming anxiety, are in a pot on the table. A peacock, a symbol of confidence, manifestation, honesty, and prosperity, sits on a fence outside the window.

Meaning: Need for self-confidence, domination by others or oneself over others, positive force overcomes anxiety, injured self-esteem, overcoming challenges, assimilating ideas, positive attitude deflects a negative situation, facing one's own limitations, personal courage needed to persevere, opposition to ideas or plans, reprioritize for success, forcefulness to achieve goals, facing adversaries.

Reversed: Vacillations, spitefulness, empty gains, stagnation from fear of defeat.

Prompt Words: Need self-confidence.

Six of Athames

This card shows steady progress is being made and a difficult time is passing. The person is moving toward smoother waters, leaving worries and upsets behind. There is a sense of peace of mind and tranquility, yet there could be a feeling of sadness that things did not work out as originally anticipated. This may be especially true if a physical move or change of employment is indicated in the reading. This card can also represent a journey with positive results for alleviating current problems, worries, or dangers. Because the change may be imposed due to circumstances beyond one's control, there may be a sense of loss, of having to leave something behind. Nevertheless, this is a positive and ultimately soothing transition, whether physical, material, emotional, or intellectual. Things will improve, and soon there will be a feeling of relief and hope for a better future. Conflicts are being left behind and one is moving to calmer waters. Victory over adversity is handled with dignity, and may stem from having made a decision with calm consideration. A difficult time is passing, and troubles are being left behind. There is a much-needed break from troubles, and time alone or with close family or friends to sort things out and make plans for future goals. This is also a card of vacations and travels, possibly overseas.

Mustard, for travel, money, protection, and strength, grows on the riverbank. The horse, a symbol of travel, cooperation, power, and renewal, stands beside the traveler.

Meaning: Steady progress, improvement, overcoming difficulties, sorting things out, troubles left behind, a tranquil journey, success after worries and anxieties, new opportunities, sacrifices bring success.

Reversed: Turmoil, displacement, delays, unable to get away from problems, need to handle turbulent situation.

Prompt Words: Steady progress, leaving troubles behind.

Seven of Athames

This card indicates that prudent planning brings success despite opposition to plans. There are dangers in the lonely forest, but the hunter's mental alertness and courage see him through. He has a sense of calm and humor that allows nothing to deter him. He is a good provider, and the woman in the doorway stands with ladle in hand and a fire ready for cooking, for she knows the hunter will succeed.

A clever approach to challenges to one's plans will overcome resistance. Self-reliance is also suggested, with the understanding that one cannot depend on others to clear the way for new ideas and new approaches to problems. Self-confidence and strategy show the mental acuity and perception that will see a plan through to completion. This is a card of using tactical skills to surmount any blockages to one's plans. This card may appear in matters dealing with corporate, legal, military, and competitive careers, showing that one has the edge over rivals and opponents through shrewd intellect and self-assurance. The odds against achieving one's goals may be surmounted through cunning and skillful guile. Diplomacy and creative thinking may be factors, but the emphasis is on indirect action rather than confrontation. Presenting ideas tactfully offers a better chance of success, and requires an agile mind. One may get the drop on the opposition, disarming arguments ahead of any public discussion, leaving them unprepared.

Ferns represent confidence, defense, security, and well-being. A polecat, a symbol of confidence, determination, independence, and willpower, waddles toward the underbrush.

Meaning: Using strategy and creativity, self-confidence, diplomacy, tact, success through perseverance, creative action forces change, new plans, fortitude, cunning, guile, clever approach to opposition, disarming opponents with mental skill.

Reversed: Betrayal, timid, fearful, delayed action, deceit, plans frustrated, indecision, quarrels.

Prompt Words: Strategy, clever approach.

Eight of Athames

In this card the woman is safe where she stands, although she doesn't know which way to go. This could be an initiation test, a prelude to trusting intuition or others who may guide her. But for now, this card is saying that there is no need to make a decision or change. Get more information or let things evolve for a while, and then one will know which way to go. Although things may seem futile at present, the way will become clear. There is no need to struggle or make a hasty decision or choice. Instead, stay the course, and as things unfold, one will be able to discern the best path to take. Patience is implied with this card, knowing that there is light after the storm, and current confusion will soon pass of its own accord. With attention to detail and gathering information, current difficulties will be overcome. Time is needed to resolve a situation or find an answer to a dilemma. Sometimes this card can relate to time needed to recover from illness.

Apples, for challenge, decisions, self-discipline, and insight, are in the tree and on the ground. A hedgehog, a symbol of concentration, resourcefulness, and intuition, is walking toward the apples.

Meaning: Stay the course, take no action for now, goals temporarily obstructed, feeling trapped, ignoring reality, untrustworthy gossip, information gathered for resolution of problem, frustration, improved health requires time.

Reversed: Self-imposed restrictions, hasty action regretted.

Prompt Words: Stay the course, patience is needed.

Nine of Athames

This is a card of stress, worry, and anxiety usually without a basis in reality. The woman awakes at night filled with the unfounded fears of a nightmare. But this will pass and things will be brighter in the morning. The card may suggest that the stress comes from worrying about the problems of other people (especially those close to one) that those people need to solve. Overly sensitive or empathic people may carry the worries of others so these become their own burden without resolution. This card warns one to relax and not get worked up over matters that will be sorted out with time or that are not one's own problem. One needs to release the fears and worries.

It is important to remember that the visions of terror and worse-case scenarios are dreams, not reality. This card shows an overly active imagination with negative thoughts predominating, and this predisposition needs to be controlled by the individual. One needs to meet those fears head-on, using the intellect to take control and turn the negative feelings into positive action to avert the envisioned problems. One is advised not to dwell on an unhappy situation, but to realize that it will pass, and there is strength in reserve to bring plans to fruition and alleviate fears. Self-doubt is usually unfounded, and by sorting out the problems, one can tame the sense of foreboding and handle the situation.

Agrimony, an herb of protection, reversing negativity, and promoting sleep, is in a vase near the bed. A bat, a symbol of releasing fears, flutters outside the window.

Meaning: Needless anxiety, understanding eases worries, need to relax, plans about to be realized, overly empathetic to problems of others.

Reversed: Depressed, sad, oppressed by troubles, self-doubt.

Prompt Words: Needless anxiety, unhappy situation.

Ten of Athames

This card signifies that it is time to turn the page on a past ordeal and release the associated negativity for self-healing. It may be a matter of cutting one's losses and moving on with life, or of acknowledging past pain and suffering and recognizing that this is part of life, of being human, and although it is painful, time will bring healing. The matter could be a past emotional upset, an event that called into question one's self-esteem, or not succeeding in what was deemed important, yet one has survived and can now heal by letting it go. Forgiving or blessing the cause or source of the pain tells the mind that the matter is over and no longer need occupy one's thoughts or drain one's energy. Now it is time to move forward and once more prove one's abilities and talents.

This card may imply that a problem is solved or a stressful situation is passing. With an impartial assessment and careful deliberation, one may succeed at surmounting a difficulty after an initial fear of failure. Through courage and willpower, things will improve, and there may be an extreme change in one's life. Wisdom is suggested, for one learns through the lessons of life, and things will improve after this period passes.

Mandrake root, for healing, overcoming challenges, and banishing negativity, is being wrapped in a cloth. One of the boars, symbols of healing, determination, power, and protection, watches nearby.

Meaning: Difficulties end, a new future awaits, putting a bad situation behind, proving one's abilities and talents, careful deliberation, troubles conquered, honest assessment of a situation, the worst is over, able to complete a difficult task.

Reversed: Exhaustion, disappointment, fear of ruin, unworkable ideas.

Prompt Words: End of present troubles, time to look forward instead of backward.

Page of Athames

This is a card of the apprentice who is eager to test the skills learned. There is an adroit use of language talents and a desire to be more self-assertive. Here the young girl practices calling the quarters for ritual, using the instructions in her Book of Shadows and gaining self-confidence with her actions. This is the beginning of independent thinking, but one must take care not to let this self-assurance slip into the cockiness of ambition and certitude. The time is right to showcase one's talents for evaluation, endorsement, recognition, or advancement. Proving oneself can be a personal matter or one related to work, with the implied caution of possible competition with others reaching for the same goal. Vigilance is needed, plus a keen awareness of learning what is required to pursue one's goals. Competitors may be engaging in spying and gossip, so one must be discreet with words and apply the necessary wisdom to avoid spitefulness. Be wary of taking inappropriate shortcuts, for there is abundant energy to get past obstructions to learning and, through the testing, to prove one's ability in pursuit of one's goals.

Borage, representing an increase of psychic power, protection, and courage, grows in the clearing. An owl, a symbol of Moon magic and intuition, watches from a nearby tree branch.

Meaning: Assertiveness, showcasing talents, demonstrating abilities for advancement, testing skills, pursuing goals, vigilance, language skills, proving abilities, scrupulous preparation, practicing a skill, beginnings of independent thinking, preparing for action.

Reversed: Spying, gossip, cunning, deceitful, unfinished projects, change of plans.

Prompt Words: Showcasing talents, vigilance.

Knight of Athames

This is a card of swift action, especially once one's mind is made up. There is determination and an aggressive approach to getting something done, so the inherent warning is to look before leaping. Spur-of-the-moment enthusiasm and the excitement of embarking on a new objective could result in a lack of preparation or making a premature commitment without a solid understanding of what is involved. There is an element of impulsiveness and a sense of self-assuredness that could border on recklessness in pursuit of adventure. However, this card indicates a smart, eager, and courageous person who is goal-focused and has the capacity to succeed with determination and incisiveness. Sudden changes are possible, as well as the skill to solve one's own problems. Impatience and a quick temper may hinder cooperation from others; however, this card indicates someone who is competent and able to take charge for a successful conclusion.

Peppermint, for action, challenges, and accomplishment, grows wild along the track. A badger, a symbol of assertiveness, determination, and action, watches from one side of the track.

Meaning: Swift action, aggressive energy, self-assured, sudden changes, boldness, courage, ability, skill, incisive career activity, bravery, heroic action, quick implementation of ideas.

Reversed: Impulsive, impatience, boastfulness, showing off, quick temper, headstrong, impractical ideas, unprincipled in pursuit of goals.

Prompt Words: Swift action.

Queen of Athames

This is the card of an analytical, shrewd, and insightful mind at work. This is someone who carefully plans things step by step and prefers that things be done in an orderly, organized fashion. This sense of strength, independence, and idealism can lead to isolation and activities that feature self-reliance. Self-expression of the intellect through language could involve writing, scientific research, and other professional ventures. A balance is needed so that the big picture is not lost in the little details, and the tendency to micromanage every facet of a project or an objective can create tension with others involved. This card is indicative of refinement and controlled emotions, but also of an appreciation of the beauty of nature. Quick-witted and keenly insightful, this person is capable of swiftly assessing a situation or another person. The only danger here is in alienating others who fail to understand this versatile and focused mind, which could lead to loneliness or sorrow. In a reading, this card suggests that being true to oneself and retaining one's individuality is important but needs to be tempered with courtesy toward others.

Iris, for wisdom, is being carefully arranged in a vase. A goldfinch, a symbol of awakening, determination, and balance, flutters outside the window.

Meaning: Analytical, planning, keen perception, language skills, quick wit, determined, independent, focused, intellectual, aloof, perceptive, self-determined, reserved, management skills, taking action, manifesting thoughts.

Reversed: Micromanaging, impractical, suspicious, isolated, ill-tempered, narrow-minded.

Prompt Words: Analytical, insightful.

King of Athames

This is a card of legal matters, official documents, contracts, licenses, registrations, and documents requiring signatures and authentication. Associated with the legal profession or inventive creativity, this card shows the application of authority and power blended with the will to act. Shrewdness and honesty are implied, along with direct and precise speech. The drawback is that a tendency toward tyranny can evolve from one's forceful certainty of being right. Personal analytical ability and the intellectual pursuit of being a recognized authority in a field of endeavor can encourage an authoritarian attitude. Because authority derives from intellect, the person may seem emotionally shallow or aloof, but actually the emotions are merely subordinated to the mind in the process of making decisions and cultivating personal talents.

Through innovation and strategy, plans are put into motion for a successful conclusion. Strong leadership skills and professionalism are involved here, plus the ability to judiciously discern what is needed to get the job done and what is unimportant.

Galangal, a plant whose root represents success with justice, legal matters, and advocacy skills, grows in a large flowerpot at one side of the desk. Fireflies, symbols of power, communication, skill, and guidance, are seen outside the window.

Meaning: Legal matters, official documents, registrations, contracts, licenses, authority, innovative, career satisfaction, shrewd, decisive, use of scientific method and thought, objectivity, professionalism, ideas implemented.

Reversed: Dominating, authoritarian, severity, willful, maliciousness, selfishness, resistance to plans.

Prompt Words: Legal matters, inventive.

Wands

FIRE

career • work • creativity
energy • ambition • ventures
south • summer

Ace of Wands

This is a card of powerful energy for a new career or a new phase in one, as well as for creativity and success in one's work. The Ace of Wands represents elemental fire, incorporating the power of solar energy, creativity, growth, and drive, particularly in the area of career. Career matters may predominate, but any line of work, be it that of a homemaker, student, employee, or employer, could be indicated. Imagination and aspiration are animated into action, allowing one to pursue objectives with bright ideas and new enthusiasm for manifesting these goals. The energy is also physical, allowing for the pursuit of vision, the starting of a new career or enterprise, and the expression of life force. Passion and drive are coupled with the ability to see things through to completion. This is a card of action and invention, showing truth and an authentic new perspective. As generative energy, this card may also refer to the birth of a baby or a new project that is one's "baby." As the elemental power of fire, the Ace of Wands represents the summer months of June, July, and August for the purpose of timing in relation to other cards in a reading.

Cherries, for creativity, hope, and expectations, are seen on treetops. A wren, a symbol of activation, adaptability, and confidence, flutters close to the wand.

Meaning: New career start, new phase in career, creativity, success, new ideas, discussions, start of an enterprise, taking action, journey for career or artistic work, new initiative, adventure, enthusiasm in work, birth of a baby, new project.

Reversed: Stagnation, career delays, burdensome work, unrealized ambition, postpone decisions.

Prompt Words: New career, new career phase.

Two of Wands

This is a card of launching a new career project with a good outlook for success. Here the woman has embarked on a weaving career as a cottage industry and sends her goods to market with hope and determination for good sales. Also related to this card is the time of waiting for the results of taking a chance on something new. While the outlook is good for seeing one's personal vision become a reality, there is still a period of time before the returns are actually known. The phase of uncertainty is supported by the careful deliberation that went into beginning the project or creative endeavor. What is desired is defined, the action taken to proceed has begun, and now comes the time of waiting for the rewards. This card implies that success will come from a venture carried out with boldness and self-confidence. It is the fire of ambition coupled with the talent and determination to see it through. There could be a formulation of subsequent aims based on the results of the initial undertaking, showing the ability to apply lessons learned, hone skills, and work to achieve success.

Allspice, an herb of career, creative energy, determination, and luck, grows in containers by the door. Two toads, symbols of good luck, opportunity, and success, carry wands away from the cottage.

Meaning: Launching a new career project, awaiting work results, auspicious beginning, new venture, creative pursuit, seeking fulfillment, determination, sense of one's own power to achieve, good outlook for success in work, earned success, ready for new ventures.

Reversed: Unfocused plans, gains less than desired, lack of growth, dissatisfied with work results.

Prompt Words: Bold new venture.

Three of Wands

This is a card of getting better returns than expected from a career or work venture. Working in harmony with others on a business or creative undertaking ensures success, resulting in good earnings. There may have been negotiations and prior planning involved to make things move smoothly, including committee work, corporate diversity, and manufacturing contracts. Teamwork may have gotten the job done, and everyone reaps their portion of the rewards. In the card image, it took the ship captain as well as the entrepreneur, labor, industry, and the ship's crew to make this a successful trading endeavor that brought a good conclusion to their work. The three wands held by the figurehead show that others were involved in the process of achieving the aims set by one person. Even when the gain comes from investments, the practical knowledge and skills of others are important in bringing an undertaking to a successful conclusion.

A laurel, a tree of fame, prosperity, success, and manifestation, grows nearby. A rat, a symbol of determination, intelligence, success, and wealth, sits on an arriving cargo box.

Meaning: Good returns on a venture, business gains, initiative pays off better than expected, optimism, planning and teamwork ensure success, celebrating success, able to accept advice and assistance from others.

Reversed: Pride interferes with goals, impractical schemes, overly speculative.

Prompt Words: Returns on a venture are better than expected.

Four of Wands

This card represents a rewarding conclusion to a career, work, or creative effort. With the harvest comes a time of rejoicing and enjoying the fruits of one's labors. Sometimes life changes come with the security of good earnings, and this may be when weddings, parties with coworkers, or family reunions are planned to help celebrate the achievement. There is a sense of orderliness and job satisfaction, with hard work completed. It is a time to bring together all those involved with the process in joyful camaraderie. This card may also suggest a romance with someone met through a work, career, or artistic endeavor. There may be a possible elevation in work, by promotion or new assignment. A strong career foundation has been laid, providing one with a sense of stability and opening the way for romance, marriage, and family.

Blue violets, for well-being, happiness, and fidelity, are under the table. A cicada, a symbol of happiness, the home, and success, walks on the table.

Meaning: Celebration of work completed, status increase, vitality, prosperity, career success, efforts rewarded, happy home, promotion, harmony, labors end well, reaping a good harvest, security, job satisfaction, camaraderie, teamwork, revelry, stability from a venture, romance, enjoying the fruits of one's labors, ready for marriage and family.

Reversed: Minimal returns for labor, delays in completion of a project, romance fades, minor disruptions at home, disorganization, work dissatisfaction.

Prompt Words: Career celebration.

Five of Wands

This card shows the need for organization and teamwork in a career or creative activity. It can represent the initial stage of a team project, with members learning the overall requirements or individual roles. A competitive environment or personnel reorganization may prompt changes at the workplace, possibly with someone leaving or a newcomer arriving. The project it-self could be subject to changes that may unsettle people for a time, or someone might not be handling their appointed share of the workload, relying on the team to carry through. With a likely reorganization comes the opportunity to demonstrate one's leadership skills. Everyone on the team needs to know where they fit in with the project or how their assignment con-tributes to the whole. The team members need to understand the importance of their work and that it is a valued part of the whole for a successful completion of the task. Someone could be let go or promoted, causing a reshuffling of work assign-ments within the remainder of the team. There may be annoy-ances with coworkers or competition for contracts and career moves. There is an element of struggling to bring ideas into re-ality, overcoming unforeseen problems, and possible compro-mises, but there is also strength in purpose and creativity to accomplish the task.

Mullein, an herb of determination, unity, and purposeful ac-tion, sprouts next to the basket in the clearing. An ant, a symbol of discipline, order, and goals, carries off a crumb of bread.

Meaning: Competition, need for teamwork, showcase leader-ship ability, unexpected personnel changes, struggle to achieve goals, obstacles overcome by cooperation, organiza-tion solves problems, rise in status, conflict brings change in procedures or assignments.

Reversed: Stubbornness, disputes, complex problems, contra-dictions, arguments, indecisiveness.

Prompt Words: Reorganization, teamwork needed.

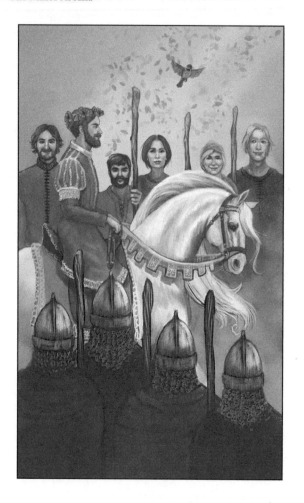

Six of Wands

This is a card of career victory and public acclaim. There may be an award, a certificate, a trophy, or praise for a job well done involved. This card could represent receiving a pay raise, bonus, or promotion for good results in achieving an important goal in one's career or in a creative project. It can also represent a personal rather than public experience wherein one has a sense of ability proven through good financial returns or praise from outside sources, as with artistic endeavors. One's self-image may be enhanced through winning or placing well in a competition, such as one involving sports, games, art, literature, or media work. There may be a prize involved or some other recognition that is meaningful to the person receiving it. The indication is of a well-earned victory in which the success is merited and others are aware of this. There may have been difficulties that needed to be surmounted to gain success and public recognition for outstanding performance.

Red poppies, for assertiveness, challenges, and support, are in the victory wreath. A sparrow, a symbol of dignity, assertiveness, loyalty, and manifestation, flies ahead of the rider.

Meaning: Victory in a career or creative enterprise, public recognition, acclaim, job well done, efforts rewarded, goals achieved after difficulties, acknowledgment, honors, advancement, successful self-expression, career goals achieved, gains from one's own efforts.

Reversed: Vanity, overestimation of one's own abilities, apprehension prevents action, insurmountable odds, need to consider plans of others.

Prompt Words: Career victory, public acclaim.

Seven of Wands

This card shows that one is able to overcome challenges or rivals in the area of career or creativity. There may be obstacles in the way of success or a need to stand up for a principle, yet one is able to accomplish the work. This card may indicate that one does things differently than established procedure, but the inventive process works. One is able to surmount difficulties to be in a better position, above the competition and testing and able to prevail over rivals and secure a good career position. Although working against the odds, one is well suited for self-defense and achieving the desired results. Sometimes this card refers to being in a superior career position despite criticism from others. There may be a need to defend one's position or ideas, utilizing all the natural instincts and skills gained through experience. This card also relates to the efforts of a writer, student, or teacher in getting ideas across to others.

Purple columbines, flowers of courage and resolve to overcome difficulties, are set on the mantle. A nuthatch, a symbol of courage, manifestation, and self-confidence, sits in a hazel tree outside the window.

Meaning: Overcoming challenges, beating the odds, trusting intuition and instinct, maintaining self-confidence, success, advantage, keeping problems under control methodically, pushing for one's own ideas, facing and managing issues as they appear.

Reversed: Self-doubt, attention diverted from problems, embarrassment, need to accept assistance, need to conform to established procedures.

Prompt Words: Advantage, defending a position, courage.

Eight of Wands

This is a card of good career news coming swiftly. The news can be from a distance, a reply to a résumé or application, or it could be good results from a creative or career venture. One is able to make sudden progress in such an endeavor, or there is an unexpected breakthrough or advancement coming. If the news has not yet arrived at the time of the reading, it should arrive within a few days. This is a card of swift progress and plans having the confirmation to proceed. Here is a possible resolution to problems, and a period of activity follows. While the events may be short-term, or there may be some travel involved, the view is one of optimism, as when an impasse is finally broken and things start moving again. There is progress and even possible advancement as a result. The caution here is to avoid making a hasty decision that might afford only a temporary solution without laying the foundation for long-term gains.

Scotch broom, for action, communication, purpose, and prosperity, is being gathered. A black-crested titmouse, a symbol of activation, knowledge, and good cheer, has settled on the blanket.

Meaning: News or communication coming soon from a distance, sudden progress, swift action for advancement, travel, period of waiting ending, events gain speed, tensions resolved, plans allowed to proceed, progress may be quick but not permanent.

Reversed: Deception, journey canceled or delayed, hasty decision is impractical, postponements, quarrels, creative tensions.

Prompt Words: News from a distance, swift action.

Nine of Wands

This card shows that one has job security but does not believe it. As a result, one is territorial and defensive about work, always alert to others trying to take credit for what one has accomplished. There may have been past difficulties or experiences where one felt slighted or betrayed by coworkers, and now one's defenses are up. Suspicious of the motives of others, one is cautious and prepared for trouble whether it comes or not, yet career success is in the making. The desire is to take responsibility for the work completed and succeed without the interference of coworkers. There is a fortification built out of solid ability and expertise, with the energy and strength to handle any problems that may arise. Past success has been noticed or praised, generating competition and envy from others. But one is in a state of readiness, with the inner determination to succeed and deal decisively with any opposition as a project nears completion. It may be necessary to make adjustments to plans or to overcome some objections to complete a project.

Bluebells, plants of abundance, attachments, and fear, grow in the yard. A mole, a symbol of awareness, sensitivity, and guardedness, digs near the fence.

Meaning: Territorial, job security, defensive about work position, able to succeed, strength in adversity, seizing opportunities, career power, anticipating difficulties, suspicious of motives, prepared to deal with challenges in career or creative work.

Reversed: Impracticality, obstinacy, uncertainties.

Prompt Words: Job security earned, defensiveness.

Ten of Wands

This card shows that one is carrying a heavy workload but has pride in accomplishment. The indication is one of a microman-ager, someone who prefers to do all the work because others are not trusted to get things right. There are aspects of the work that could be delegated, but one is reluctant to do so, due to either pride or distrust of another's ability. If the load becomes too oppressive, the work can still be shared, but one needs to accept that it may not be up to one's exceptionally high standards and perhaps may even reflect something of the personalities of those who help. With this type of attitude, a person may actually work below a job description, such as when a supervisor does the work of a clerk to ensure it is done right. This could have a negative impact on a person when performance reviews are conducted. This card can also reflect the desire to handle all aspects of a job for the satisfaction of overcoming a personal challenge. One has the gratification of achieving an objective on one's own terms. This card can also suggest that once one has learned to handle a job well, the lack of challenge makes it feel burdensome. There is also the tendency to become overbearing because of the need for continuing success.

Dill, a plant representing stress, security, fortitude, and willpower, grows along the path. A squirrel, a symbol of concentration, action, and knowledge, watches nearby.

Meaning: Carrying a burden, need to delegate, determination to achieve goals, stressful work pressures.

Reversed: Overcommitted, plans halted, burdensome success.

Prompt Words: Heavy workload, pride in accomplishment.

Page of Wands

This is a card of career restlessness. A person may be looking around to see what else is out there in one's field of interest, but there is no immediate change in the works. Here the lad is on his way to market with baskets full of thyme to sell. This is the perhaps the first time he has gone alone, and he makes a circle of protection to ensure his travels are safe. Exploring new territory and picking up new responsibilities are implied in this card, setting the stage for later change. A person may send out résumés or applications to test the waters, but there is not a sense of certitude about how to respond to answers. There is new creativity or career experience that creates a desire for expression and agitation for action. Important news may be coming, perhaps relating to the completion of a project. Creative potential and inspiration require nurturing and tentative application to determine what are reliable and usable ideas. This youthful energy offers spontaneity and the desire to see things through to completion. Ambition coupled with resourcefulness is energized for successful action through a person who is consistent and trustworthy.

Thyme, representing confidence, growth, and skills, is gathered in the baskets. A donkey, a symbol of courage, opportunity, awakening wisdom, and learning, carries the load.

Meaning: Restlessness, new creative inspiration, new ideas, honorable intentions, loyalty, honesty, important news, self-reliant, independent action, creating long-term plans.

Reversed: Impatience, petty rivalries, flattery from a false friend, easily influenced.

Prompt Words: Career restlessness, resourceful, important news.

Knight of Wands

This card signifies that a new career adventure is starting with lots of energy and enthusiasm. Here the woman is riding to a village to either look for work or begin a new job. One takes talent, skills, creativity, and knowledge to another level with optimism and confidence. There is an eagerness to embrace all that life has to offer, and there may be a journey involved or even a change of residence. One advances fearlessly into the unknown, hoping to fulfill the call of ambition and expansion. This card could relate to striking out on a new career or artistic endeavor, résumé and recommendations in hand, or one could experience advancement in current work that takes one to a higher level or involves relocation.

Things have been thought out prior to making the move, thus supporting one's self-assurance with practical insight. Departures or absences due to work may be in effect as well, although this could also imply that one is unafraid to dive into a whole new career or creative expression, such as quitting one job to take another in a different field. Other cards in the spread may indicate if this is a total change requiring additional training or if one is taking known skills elsewhere or into a new project in the same job. Imminent career or creative opportunities await, and one is charging ahead in pursuit.

Goldenseal, for strength, stimulation, wisdom, and prosperity, is in the wreath. A nighthawk, a symbol of freedom, determination, and success, flies overhead.

Meaning: Energetic ambition, time of action, adventurer, new experiences, new career or creative venture starting, enthusiasm, journey, departure, change of residence, opportunities, exploring the unknown, fearlessness, dynamic and rapid action.

Reversed: Disorganized travel, looking for new employment, interrupted activity, jealousy at the workplace.

Prompt Words: New career enterprise.

Queen of Wands

This card relates to being practical and channeling energy automatically. There is a need to release any negativity to prevent it from interfering with work, creativity, or personal relationships. Good-natured kindness is indicated, along with the characteristics of dependability, faithfulness, and loyalty. There is also a sense of self-mastery and self-confidence, as well as a warm personality. This card may represent a friendly confidant or someone who is easy to talk to and a good listener who can offer sound advice. One's creative vision extends to all facets of life with warmth and optimism, and energy is put to work joyfully yet is tempered with understanding. This card could indicate a person who is imaginative and sincere as well as self-actualized and empowered, and as such is willing to help others. Creativity and a keen mind are indicated here, as well as a loving nature and attachment to home.

Hyacinth, for kindness, optimism, and happiness, is in a vase on the bench. A golden oriole, a symbol of optimism, energy, and enjoyment of life, is in the bush.

Meaning: Optimistic, practical, sincere, loyal, creative, kindly, eloquent, insightful, expressive, imaginative, clever, self-confident, channeling energy, independent, strong-willed, good planner, gracious, friendly.

Reversed: Critical, irritable, jealous, insecure, unconfident.

Prompt Words: Practical, channeling energy.

King of Wands

This is the card of a wise counselor or advisor, a respected leader or professional in a scientific, academic, or medical field. This is someone who has good intentions and is willing to share knowledge with others for their benefit. This person may be giving honest advice and direction with one's best interests at heart. This could be a business consultant, a project collaborator, an instructor, or a professional in a career or a creative field. A paternal, sympathetic outlook may be implied, with a desire to be of help to others. This card can indicate a career in an academic area, or a school counselor who advises on requirements that need to be met, helps one gather necessary documents for further education or career advancement, or assigns courses that will lead one to fulfill an education or training goal. This shows that professional cooperation helps one to achieve the best results in a venture or career. Being assertive, but with sincerity, one may present new ideas to be initiated and find acceptance by others. This card may also indicate a liaison, a discreet go-between of good character and reputation. There are good relationships and a conscientious effort at maintaining them, although actions are sometimes taken arising from impulse.

Lemon balm, an herb of comfort, career, success, and sympathy, is in the flowerpot. A ferret, a symbol of gentleness, ingenuity, and security, plays with the edge of the robe.

Meaning: Assertive, professional, counselor, advisor, mentor, honest, conscientious, learned, able to bring ideas to fruition, good counsel, good relations, spiritual attainment, educated, refined, respected teacher, self-assured, living the ideal of truth and enlightenment, cooperation.

Reversed: Austere, dogmatic, critical, thoughtless actions, difficult deliberations.

Prompt Words: Counselor, knowledgeable.

Chalices

WATER

emotions • psychic ability
fulfillment • relationships
west • autumn

Ace of Chalices

This is a card of love, joy, happiness, and abundance. One's cup overflows with emotional satisfaction, and the light of the Sun emphasizes the positive energy being transmitted. The power of elation is so great as to offer nourishment to others. This is also a card of productivity and fulfillment, possibly indicating fertility or pregnancy. One can act with determination, knowing the result will be satisfying. As a symbol of elemental water, this card incorporates the lunar forces of the subconscious mind, enhancing psychic ability and moving the emotional tides within one. This is a power card of beneficial aspect offering happiness in relationships and unity with the Divine through love. As it is related to the influence of the Moon, trust in the power of intuition is also indicated. The warning here is not to let one's emotions turn into affectation with exaggerated or dramatized feelings to the point where they are perceived as insincere or pretentious. As the elemental power of water, the Ace of Chalices represents the autumn months of September, October, and November for the purpose of timing in relation to other cards in a reading.

Honeysuckle, for abundance, love, happiness, and fidelity, blooms around the chalice. A salmon, a symbol of abundance, guidance, and endurance, leaps from the river.

Meaning: Abundance, joy, love, fulfillment, inspiration, fount of life, productive, psychic ability, overflowing happiness, important relationship, positive change, contentment, fertility, possible pregnancy, perfection, satisfaction.

Reversed: Emotionalism, upsets, delays, unrequited love.

Prompt Words: Abundance, joy.

Two of Chalices

This is a card of good communication and loving companionship. A true lover's card, it shows that a choice or decision has been made and that a couple is well suited for each other. It may also represent a congenial relationship between two people, and while usually reflecting love, understanding, and possibly marriage, it can also apply simply to a satisfying partnership in a business, friendship, or social setting where there is a strong bond between two people. There may be a happy surprise, a proposal, or a reconciliation implied. As this is a card of joy and happiness, the relationship may be clarified by the surrounding cards in a spread. There is a sense of well-being that is shared with another, with mutual respect and enjoyment. Creative ideas may also be indicated, shared, and appreciated by another who is close. Agreement and an agreeable relationship bring one comfort and security. There is a strong bond of trust here, as well as dependability and goodwill.

Coriander, a plant of love, fidelity, home, happiness, peace, and security, grows near the couple. A goose, a symbol of fidelity, love, communication, and comfort, watches nearby.

Meaning: Emotional balance, good communication, satisfying partnership, compatibility, proposal, harmony, reconciliation, cooperation, affinity, affection, a happy surprise.

Reversed: Emotional misunderstandings, disunion, ending a relationship, self-indulgence, unappreciative of another.

Prompt Words: Good partnership, harmony.

Three of Chalices

This is a card of celebration, of getting together with people one likes for a joyful occasion such as a birthday, wedding, baby shower, anniversary, or other important event. This card can also reflect the Triple Goddess theme of Maiden, Mother, and Crone, with the three aspects united as one, thus representing unity. There is also a sense of flexibility and good work relations indicated, possibly with good news that makes one cheerful. If there had been illness, there is likely healing energy involved. There is good fortune and the desire to share this joy with others. The pleasure of companionship may be calm and quiet or more boisterous, as with a party atmosphere. Often there is a specific social event in the works, such as a family gathering for an engagement, marriage, or birth. The event is mutually well received and happy, so the card may show that past issues have been successfully resolved, bringing new optimism and a sharing of good times. A good conclusion to a matter brings fulfillment and warrants a social celebration.

Water lilies, plants of happiness and connections, are in the pond. A pheasant, a symbol of harmony, confidence, and warmth, flies overhead.

Meaning: Joyful occasion, fulfillment, celebration, wedding, birthday, anniversary, healing, vitality, good news, happy outcome, party, good fortune, relief, problem resolved, optimism.

Reversed: Self-indulgent, excesses, unappreciated.

Prompt Words: Celebration, special occasion.

Four of Chalices

This is a card of dissatisfaction despite current success. Although one has sufficient emotional well-being, one is seeking something more. There is a sense of restlessness and of looking for greener pastures, perhaps due to satiation, too much of a good thing. One desires something new to feel revitalized. One may need to reassess one's situation to be able to reach out to a prospect for greater fulfillment. Such an opportunity will not fall into one's lap, so one must make the effort to seize it to accomplish what is desired. There may be a need to reevaluate a relationship or assess an unexpressed yearning that remains in a faithful commitment. It is this self-exploration of what will bring greater emotional satisfaction that is tinged with a latent longing to know if the right choices have been made and if what one has attained is genuine. Even with external needs being well met, internal contentment is being questioned. This may signal a new direction in emotional expression so that a sense of balance, symbolized by the Three of Chalices instead of the Four, returns.

Dittany, an herb of desires, beginnings, and manifestation, grows in a flowerpot. A dragonfly, a symbol of guidance, activation, and inspiration, flies into the room.

Meaning: Discontent, dissatisfaction, opportunity to achieve a goal requires action, need for reassessment, stationary period, new approach to old problems comes, satiation, new possibilities, faithfulness, new friendships, need for new challenges, unidentified longings, motivation needed.

Reversed: Boredom, apathy, seeking mindless distractions, aversion, troublesome relations.

Prompt Words: Opportunity to end dissatisfaction.

Five of Chalices

This is a card of old emotional upsets, sorrow, and regrets. The time has come to release them and move on with one's life. Instead of focusing on the unhappy past, one should acknowledge the good things in one's life and go forward with hope and optimism. Attention has been focused on emotional losses and disappointments rather than the emotional support and benefits still in reserve. A drawback to this is that after a time, others will start to avoid being around a person who continues to dwell on the past and ignores the good in the present. In some way one needs to understand that the matter is water under the bridge, the fire is out, and others do not want to hear about it anymore. Fortunately, this is usually a card of transitory mourning for something lost, with the hope of better things to come. There may be some type of emotional disappointment or hurt feelings that need to be faced and released so better things can enter one's sphere of influence. Sometimes there is a problem with an inheritance, or squabbles over a legacy among relatives.

Blackberry brambles, for attachments, grief, healing, and growth, are nearby. A hare, symbolizing crossroads, cycles, sensitivity, and renewal, watches nearby.

Meaning: Useless regrets, partial loss, difficulties with a legacy, stressful relationships, dwelling on past upsets, ignoring present bounty.

Reversed: Difficulties overcome, change in lifestyle, sharing abundance, new alliances, hopeful outlook.

Prompt Words: Useless regrets, release past upsets.

Six of Chalices

This is a card of nostalgia, remembering, and making happy memories. A reunion or an unexpected encounter with someone from the past is possible. With thoughts directed to the past, there may be an attempt to bring the comfort or ideals of the past to be realized in the present. There may be a desire to relive good memories in the present, as when a parent passes a tradition or hobby interest down to children and grandchildren, or when one attempts to repeat one's childhood in parenting. This could lead to disappointment when what was meaningful to one is not received with enthusiasm by the beneficiary. The initial disappointment could be a liberating opportunity to step beyond the wistfulness of the past and move into the reality of the present, to be able to acknowledge and appreciate the differences of others. There is both longing for the good old days and a desire to bring some of those good memories into the present, but with care and relevance to the current life. Living in the past can create a sense of melancholy, yet there may be connections to the past that can be utilized to manifest past dreams in the present.

Marjoram, an herb of happy memories, comfort, connections, and family, is carried by the girl. A canary, a symbol of companionship, happiness, and harmony, is carried in a cage by the boy.

Meaning: Longings, happy memories, harmony, reminiscence, reunions, expectations manifested, self-analysis, renewal.

Reversed: Melancholy, resisting change, rude awakenings.

Prompt Words: Happy memories, reunions.

Seven of Chalices

There are many opportunities or choices open to a person with this card, but not all of them are what they seem, and other people may try to influence the decision one makes. The caution is against the tendency to daydream, rely on others for direction in life, or wish for things without expending the effort to bring them to fruition. One needs to learn more about the choices offered, and pick the one that pulls. Of all the options, only one is right for the chooser, and the others are delusions. To be happy with the decision made, one must listen to the intuition and heart as well as the intellect. Here is a chance to do what will make one happy, and this may require standing up to others who wish to push their own choices, based on their personal perceptions and values. To find the true path to reaching a desired goal, one must evaluate the alternatives, look past the obstacles and distractions, and avoid following the whims or uncertain promptings of others.

Solomon's seal (drop berry), an herb of decisions, wisdom, and success, grows beside the stand. A butterfly, a symbol of opportunities, confidence, and manifestation, flutters over one chalice.

Meaning: Many choices, opportunities, careful decision, deliberations, willpower to achieve goals, time to follow one's true desire.

Reversed: Daydreams, delusion, self-deception, confusion, hesitancy, false promises, improbable ideas, whims.

Prompt Words: Opportunities, choose carefully.

Eight of Chalices

This card indicates leaving familiar surroundings and people for another location or group. This can mean a journey for career or personal development, a physical move, or a change or promotion in work or career that elevates one to a higher level and requires a change in socializing patterns. It is also a card of scholarship, showing that one is elevating one's intellectual, professional, or spiritual development, moving to a higher level and leaving behind those who fail to progress. This is a turning point in one's life, a change that may signify ending an emotionally draining or abusive situation, no longer being a willing emotional victim of others, or ceasing to be the one who does all the giving and receives nothing in return. In this sense, there is also a new understanding taking hold in which a person realizes there is no sense in continuing with the current situation. The time has come to take the lessons learned and move on. This usually means that one has abandoned some plan or project, or that one is ending a relationship, either personal or professional, for one's own good or through promotion and earned success. This card indicates that one has outgrown associates and old companions and needs to find emotional satisfaction through personal fulfillment and a new environment.

Grapes, for clarity, growth, inspiration, and mental power, grow by the beach. A cormorant, a symbol of transformation, skills, and independence, stands on a stump nearby drying its wings.

Meaning: Turning point, abandoning plans, new path, scholarship, advancement, moving to a higher level, changing social patterns.

Reversed: Dissatisfaction, reckless abandonment, forced changes.

Prompt Words: Turning point, new path.

Nine of Chalices

This is commonly called the "wish card," and it signifies that the energy is there for one's wishes to be brought into reality and for a happy future. A fortuitous card, it shows that one's intuition is accurate and one need only think about what is desired and speak it to the universe for it to manifest. The extraordinary alignment of circumstance and good decision-making brings one emotional fulfillment and satisfaction. Usually this card appears to offer reassurance to the doubter that plans can indeed be realized and that things will work out. As such, this is a card of hope as well as success and joy. It also alerts one to a beneficial alignment of energies that can be utilized before it moves on, for energy is always in motion. Life is about to improve, and by following that which intuitively attracts one, success will be attained. Good health is indicated, and improvement in one's circumstances is coming with abundance and success. Efforts are rewarded and wishes are fulfilled, so prosperity and happiness result.

Bay leaves, herbs of wishes granted, promotion, and divination, are on the mantle. A ladybug, a symbol of good luck, wishes, happiness, and divination, is on the crystal ball.

Meaning: Wishes granted, happy future, satisfaction, success, happiness, prosperity, efforts rewarded, victory, material and emotional attainment, accurate intuition, fulfillment of a dream.

Reversed: Poor choices, selfish desires, irresponsibility, self-indulgence, complacency

Prompt Words: Wishes granted, happy future.

Ten of Chalices

This is a card of family happiness, love, and abundance. The family is incorporated into the realization of personal achievement. Others recognize one's success, so a good reputation and a strong social standing are also factors.

Complete emotional contentment and stability are shared with loved ones, and life is filled with meaning and purpose. There is an ongoing and permanent happiness based upon the firm foundation of knowing what has spiritual value to one. Family well-being and a sense of connectedness are enjoyed and nurtured with love that is offered and reciprocated. Depending on other cards in the reading, there could be a pregnancy or a newcomer to the family, perhaps through marriage, adoption, or some other relationship. Home is also a place for rest and recuperation, where one may recharge after difficulties and find comfort in loving surroundings. Embracing this emotional support reflects sincerity and spoken appreciation and honor.

Clumps of asters, for unconditional love, happiness, and calm, grow in abundance. An otter, a symbol of happiness, fidelity, and joy, watches from the water.

Meaning: Love, joy, happiness in the home life, enjoying family and friends, security, contentment, recognition, social standing, reaping the rewards of efforts, satisfying emotional commitments, well-earned self-esteem.

Reversed: Family disputes, instability, endangered reputation, loss of friendship, quarrels, interrupted peace, family instability.

Prompt Words: Happiness, family contentment, security.

Page of Chalices

This is a card of creativity and deciding how to apply it. There is inspiration and a desire to put it to use. Artistic, musical, literary, or psychic abilities need an outlet, and one may be considering taking classes or focusing more on these talents with the possibility of later making a career change. There may be an invitation or offer coming, as well as new plans in the making. As representative of a person, this card shows a trustworthy and loyal companion, a friend who can be counted on to consider matters before taking action. New talents are put into practical use so that the overall feeling is one of serenity and competence in the face of change. A child may have artistic skills or developing psychic ability that can be nurtured with understanding and support. This card may indicate a new relationship beginning or a current one entering a new phase.

Purple heather, for learning, beauty, creative work, and spiritual development, is laid out on the rock. A beaver, a symbol of creativity with available resources and with setting goals, works upriver.

Meaning: Creativity, inspiration, using talents, practical use of skills, new relationship or new phase of a current relationship, artistic or other creative expression, psychic ability, new social contacts, deliberation.

Reversed: Distraction, indiscretion, superficial attraction.

Prompt Words: Creativity, finding an outlet for inspiration.

Knight of Chalices

This is a card of proposals and invitations, of socializing, networking, and making new contacts. There may be an artistic or romantic proposal, or simply the enjoyment of good times, perhaps with an invitation received to attend a propitious occasion. The invitation may allow for social advancement or provide a desired opportunity to make the necessary contacts for emotional fulfillment and satisfaction in life. If representative of a person, this card is someone who has something beneficial to offer. One's enthusiasm may prompt openings and opportunities, especially through casual mingling among people who prove helpful. Relaxation and good times are indicated, as well as holiday fun with others, and opportunities. Artistic expression is given direction and finesse. There is also a possible opportunism with this card: someone being capricious with one's emotions, vacillating and leading one on. Flattery or deception could come into play, or a person could be misleading one either for his or her own gain or simply because of an inability to be emotionally consistent or make a sincere commitment. Other cards in the spread will clarify the intention.

Marigolds, flowers of well-being, affection, and relationships, make a wreath. A stork, a symbol of beginnings, devotion, and opportunities, stands by the tree.

Meaning: Artistic direction, romantic or social proposal, invitation, fun, relaxation, opportunity, advancement, emotional sensitivity, developing style, love, breakthrough.

Reversed: Insincerity, flattery, false friend, deception, opportunistic cooperation, conniving, fraudulent schemes.

Prompt Words: Proposals, socializing.

Queen of Chalices

This is a card of empathy and a compassionate nature. One may be vulnerable to sad stories and relate overly to the problems of other people. Always having a shoulder for others to cry on can drain one's own energy and create distress and worry where none is actually warranted. One is likely to feel confused by being relied upon by another in a time of emotional crisis and then ignored once the matter has passed or been resolved. There is an inherent warning not to empathize to the point where one in sympathy reveals personal information to another who may use it against one after things are back to normal. There is also a need to be careful not to overreact to minor issues. One knows better, but has difficulty controlling the impulse to act against one's own best interests. Facing one's true feelings affords one the opportunity to make an honest assessment of what emotions and mindset drive one. There is a nurturing, loving intellect indicated by this card, and this needs to be guarded to avoid being injured by those less sensitive.

Hibiscus, a flower for psychic awareness, sensitivity, and passion, is in the queen's wreath. A crab, a symbol of emotions, sensitivity, and creativity, crawls out of the sea.

Meaning: Empathy, sympathetic, good confidant, trust feelings, insightful, artistic, psychic ability, fairness, romantic, loving, authenticity of emotions.

Reversed: Unreliable, self-centered, moody, changeable, emotionally ambivalent.

Prompt Words: Sensitivity, nurturing, empathetic.

King of Chalices

This is a card of competence, business talks, and professional assistance offered in a casual atmosphere. There is confidence through success, and security through accumulated wisdom and respect gained from others. Willing to share this expertise and acting as a mentor, counselor, or tutor, especially in a professional or business field, the person may be a compassionate healer or physician. Offering loyalty to others who may or may not reciprocate in kind, the person may be viewed as crafty and egotistical. Scientific work is also indicated, as well as interest in the creative arts. Such a person is responsible and liberal but also protective and kind. This card can also represent a business lunch with someone senior, where helpful information may be gathered. A social invitation with a business aspect may not be something one is inclined to accept, but the energy suggests it would be in one's best interests to attend. There is an opportunity for gaining face time with higher-ups, networking, making contacts, and gathering useful information. The caution is to not overindulge during the gathering so as to be able to take best advantage of one's time for self-improvement.

Globe thistle, for connections, empowerment, independence, and confidence, is in the vase. Bees, symbols of abundance, connections, power, and support, hover near the vase.

Meaning: Arts and sciences, professional, reliable counselor, considerate, giving advice, loyalty and commitment to others, business-related social invitation.

Reversed: Changeable, sly, unjust, self-serving, obstructionist.

Prompt Words: Business socializing, reliable counsel.

Chapter Three

Spreads

Spreads are used to link the cards in a pattern that helps tell a story or provide a complete picture of a situation for a meaningful interpretation. Blending the meaning of a card with the meanings of the surrounding cards during a reading will show nuances, sequences of events, energy influences, and attitudes. Surrounding cards may mitigate, explain, clarify, or add meaning to another card. More cards can be added for further information around a card that seems questionable. If another question comes out from the reading, the reader can reshuffle the remaining cards and lay out three to nine cards for a response. After reading the spread, a look at the bottom card of the deck will offer a view of the energies prominent in the querent's aura, the energy being transmitted to surrounding people, which may be something to modify if needed through affirmations or meditation.

Having mostly major arcana in a spread indicates powerful cosmic forces at work; mostly court cards shows a strong influence from other people; mostly minor arcana shows a focus on daily affairs; and having three to four aces, or three aces and the Witch, shows powerful elemental forces at work in daily life. Refer to the multiples list in the introduction for additional insights when three to four of the same numbered pips, aces, or court cards appear in a reading. The following spreads show various patterns for laying out the cards after they have been knocked on, shuffled, cut, and restacked, ready for the reading.

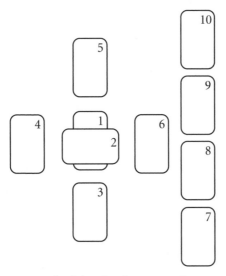

Witch's Circle Spread

1: current situation

2: current influences

3: foundation of situation

4: passing influences

5: coming influences (within three months)

6: future influences (three to six months)

7: environment

8: strengths and advantages

9: thoughts and concerns

10: outcome

Card 10 (outcome) usually relates to card 6 (future influences). Sometimes cards 7–10 show a succession of events or an evolving situation in detail, depending on the impressions received by the reader.

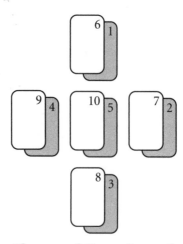

Elemental Cross Spread

Ask about a matter or choice. Lay out cards 1–5 facedown. Lay out cards 6–10 face up on top of those. Read cards 6–10 first.

    6: the matter in the physical realm

    7: the matter in the mental realm

    8: the matter in the energetic realm

    9: the matter in the emotional realm

10: the heart of the matter

Read cards 1–5 next, turning over the cards as they are read.

    1: the hidden influence of the matter in the physical realm

    2: the hidden influence of the matter in the mental realm

    3: the hidden influence of the matter in the energetic realm

    4: the hidden influence of the matter in the emotional realm

    5: the hidden heart of the matter

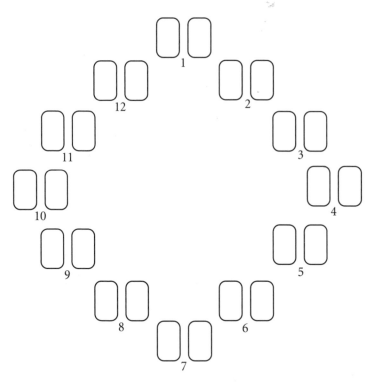

Wheel of the Year Spread

Divide the cards into two stacks and set them facedown on the table next to each other. The stack on the left indicates a major influence; the one on the right is a major event. Turn over the top card from each stack and interpret them for the first month of the year. Proceed to the next month, reading the next cards from each stack. Continue through a twelve-month cycle to see the main influence and main event for each month of the coming year. Make a chart listing the cards and meanings for each month and check this as the year passes to see how the card energies manifested.

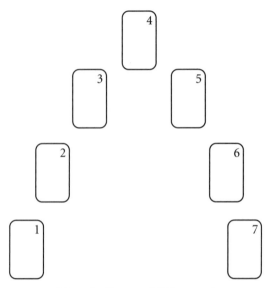

Mystic Pyramid Spread

1: past

2: present

3: near future

4: mindset

5: others' attitudes

6: obstacles

7: anticipated outcome

When uncertain about making a decision, focus on the problem and lay out the cards. The past shows the background of the matter, the present shows the situation as it currently stands, and the future shows how things might progress without making a choice. Card 4 offers insight into one's subconscious mindset, but can also indicate what is truly on one's mind regarding making a decision. Card 5 shows how other people may respond to your decision, whether this is helpful to you or not. Card 6 indicates either potential barriers to your plans or the absence of impediments, depending on the card. Card 7 shows what can arise from the decision and dealing with other people and any issues that come up along the way.

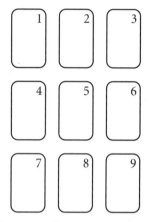

Nine-Card Square Spread

Focus on a matter or question and lay out the cards. All the cards touch upon the middle card, which is the central influence in the matter. Read the cards across as rows, down as columns, and diagonally both from right to left and left to right for a full understanding of the matter.

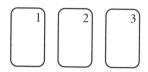

Simple Yes/No Answer Spread

Ask a question that can be answered with a yes or no.

Pull the cards to create a stack, stopping when an ace or the Witch is pulled or upon counting out the thirteenth card.

Start a second stack, stopping with an ace, the Witch, or the thirteenth card, then create a third stack the same way.

If there are three aces (or two aces and the Witch) showing, the answer is YES. If no aces or the Witch show, the answer is NO. If there are one or two aces or the Witch, the answer is POSSIBLY YES, but read the other top cards for details.

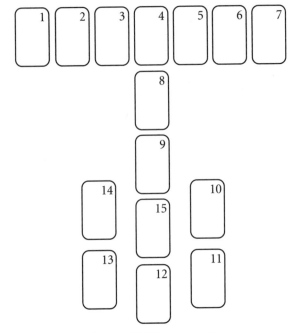

Tree of Life Spread

1–7: the branches—how the querent touches others or is touched by others; you may read these cards as pairs, from outer to inner (1 and 7, 2 and 6, 3 and 5, with 4 being the crown of the tree, indicating how others see the querent)

4: the crown of the tree—how others see the querent

4, 8, and 9: the trunk of the tree—what supports the querent

10–14: the roots—incoming energy

12: the taproot—draws the strongest energy

10, 11, 13, and 14: ancillary roots—secondary energies

15: the heart of the tree (or matter)—shows what is most important or vital

The reader may repeat the spread with more cards up to three times, reading those cards that fall together in the individual placements (1–15) for clarification or to see the progression of energies in each area.

Conclusion

Reading the cards is a joyful experience that brings us into contact and communication with the energies of the universe and the Divine Spirit that permeates it. The tarot is a tool for guidance and shows the possibilities available the way the energies are aligned. The cards do not direct or predict, but show energy alignments and offer options or choices. The reader need not feel restricted to the listed definitions, for many different things may appear in the cards to the psychic eye.

For the Witch, the tarot reveals a hidden insight into any given situation, and it is up to the individual to determine how to utilize that knowledge. Spellcasting, meditation, positive affirmations, focus, change of plans, or preparation are only some of the possible responses. The cards may help us deal wisely with an approaching energy, or be more understanding of a source of negativity, or be more able to cope with or take advantage of coming changes.

When reading for others, it is important to keep the ego in check. This is not a time to show off or make sweeping statements that might alarm, rather than assist, a querent. Be kind to others and be prudent in your language and manner by considering other ways to pass along information without being blunt. Remember to be careful with your words in a reading, for the querent may hold on to them with much greater import than you felt or intended to convey. The tarot can be an early warning system, but it is always up to the individual to heed or disregard the information drawn from the cards. The cards show potentials, not absolutes.

The images on the cards are meant to draw the reader in and to open the individual to more intuitive and channeled insights. The reader need not abide by the card descriptions offered in any book, but may rely instead on the psychic impressions received. It is not unusual for readers to start by using memorized card meanings or prompt words, only to find that after a time and with experience, the cards become a familiar tool that opens the sight to other avenues. With practice, one's confidence grows, as does one's ability to "see" where the cards point.

In all things, one must remember and abide by the Witch's rule of "harm none," and allow the tarot to open new vistas in psychic development and spiritual growth. Love is the law and love is the bond. So mote it be.

To Write the Author

If you wish to contact the author or would like more information about this book, please write to the author in care of Llewellyn Worldwide, and we will forward your request. Both the author and publisher appreciate hearing from you and learning of your enjoyment of this book and how it has helped you. Llewellyn Worldwide cannot guarantee that every letter written to the author can be answered, but all will be forwarded. Please write to:

% Llewellyn Worldwide
2143 Wooddale Drive
Woodbury, MN 55125-2989

Please enclose a self-addressed stamped envelope for reply, or $1.00 to cover costs. If outside the U.S.A., enclose an international postal reply coupon.

GET MORE AT LLEWELLYN.COM

Visit us online to browse hundreds of our books and decks, plus sign up to receive our e-newsletters and exclusive online offers.

- **Free tarot readings • Spell-a-Day • Moon phases**
- **Recipes, spells, and tips • Blogs • Encyclopedia**
- **Author interviews, articles, and upcoming events**

GET SOCIAL WITH LLEWELLYN

Find us on Facebook
www.Facebook.com/LlewellynBooks

Follow us on

www.Twitter.com/Llewellynbooks

GET BOOKS AT LLEWELLYN

LLEWELLYN ORDERING INFORMATION

Order online: Visit our website at www.llewellyn.com to select your books and place an order on our secure server.

Order by phone:
- Call toll free within the U.S. at 1-877-NEW-WRLD (1-877-639-9753)
- Call toll free within Canada at 1-866-NEW-WRLD (1-866-639-9753)
- We accept VISA, MasterCard, and American Express

Order by mail:
Send the full price of your order (MN residents add 6.875% sales tax) in U.S. funds, plus postage and handling to: Llewellyn Worldwide, 2143 Wooddale Drive Woodbury, MN 55125-2989

POSTAGE AND HANDLING

STANDARD (U.S. & Canada):
(Please allow 12 business days)
$25.00 and under, add $4.00.
$25.01 and over, FREE SHIPPING.

INTERNATIONAL ORDERS (airmail only):
$16.00 for one book, plus $3.00 for each additional book.

Visit us online for more shipping options. Prices subject to change.

FREE CATALOG!

To order, call 1-877-NEW-WRLD ext. 8236 or visit our website

GREEN WITCHCRAFT

FOLK MAGIC, FAIRY LORE
& HERB CRAFT

AOUMIEL MOURA

Green Witchcraft
Folk Magic, Fairy Lore & Herb Craft
ANN MOURA

Learn the basics of Witchcraft from a third-generation Witch raised in a family tradition. Positive, practical, and easy to use, *Green Witchcraft* brings together the best of both modern Wicca and the author's family heritage of herb craft and folk magic.

Green Witchcraft explores the fundamentals of the Wiccan religion, providing magical training for the independent thinker. Step-by-step instructions on a wide variety of magical techniques as well as basic rules of conduct make this the ideal book to get you started. Green rituals for self-initiation, rites of passage, seasonal celebrations and activities provide an excellent foundation for your own magical tradition.

Discover the fine art of spellcasting, the magical uses of herbs, divination with the tarot and more. Explore the Sabbats, Esbats, and other rituals attuned to the cycles of nature and the universal powers. Find out for yourself what this organic approach to Witchcraft is all about.

978-1-56718-690-1, 288 pp., 6 x 9   **$15.95**

GREEN WITCHCRAFT II

BALANCING
LIGHT & SHADOW

ANN MOURA
(AOUMIEL)

Green Witchcraft II
Balancing Light & Shadow
ANN MOURA

Green Witches are deeply connected to the Earth and the cosmic balance of light and dark. They welcome the wisdom of the light and the shadow sides of nature, the self, and the Divine to grow more whole in magic and spirit.

In *Green Witchcraft II*, hereditary Witch Ann Moura reveals how to develop a balanced practice by incorporating the powerful, dark aspects of the Goddess and the God. Guided meditations, spells, and rituals enable you to invoke the energy of the dark powers and achieve your goals through magical workings.

- Use dark power herbs and hear the goddess speak prophecy
- Create a connection to with the four Elementals with your own elemental bottle
- Open the doors to past-life memories with the black mirror meditation
- Learn a spell to pass easily among the three worlds
- Gather and release the chaos energy of darkness to regenerate the Earth
- Work with the dark aspects of familiars, the Celtic Ogham, and the Tarot

Honor the dark no less than the light … release your fear of the shadows and embrace the other half of yourself with the balancing practices in *Green Witchcraft II*.

978-1-56718-689-5, 264 pp., 6 x 9   **$15.95**

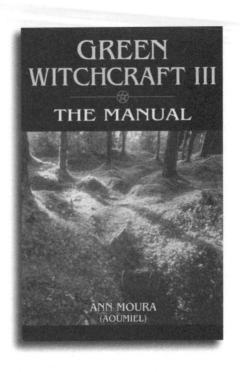

GREEN
WITCHCRAFT III
THE MANUAL

ANN MOURA
(AOUMIEL)

To order, call 1-877-NEW-WRLD
Prices subject to change without notice
Order at Llewellyn.com 24 hours a day, 7 days a week!

Green Witchcraft III: The Manual
ANN MOURA

Green Witchcraft is at the core of earth magic, the Witchcraft of the Natural Witch, the Kitchen Witch, and the Cottage Witch. It is herbal, attuned to nature, and the foundation upon which any Craft tradition may be built.

In this manual, hereditary Witch Ann Moura presents the Craft as a course of instruction, with eight magical classes that correspond to the eight Sabbats. This companion handbook to *Green Witchcraft* and *Green Witchcraft II* can also be used alone as an exploration of the Green path. Cultivate your knowledge of earth magic with the following lessons:

—Introduction to the craft, basic equipment, altars
—Casting a learning circle, meditation, and technique
—Divination with the Celtic Ogham
—Consecration of a statue, divine couples, holy days
—Divinations: crystal ball scrying, black mirror gazing
—Casting and creating spells, herb craft, candle magic
—Green rules of conduct, circle casting
—Stones and crystals, elixir preparations

Return to your roots and grow wise the ways of green magic with *Green Witchcraft III, The Manual.*

978-1-56718-688-8, 264 pp., 6 x 9   **$15.95**